Weymouth

Design Consultant: Bob Bryden, Chapel Hill, North Carolina
Photography: Seth Tice-Lewis, Chapel Hill, North Carolina
Typography: Sharon Griffith, Hillsborough, North Carolina

Front Cover: Mary Katherine Philipp—*Dogs at the Entrance to Weymouth*
Back Cover: Thomas E. Culbreth—*The Weymouth House, Southern Pines, NC*

Weymouth

An Anthology of Poetry

edited by
Sam Ragan

The St. Andrews Press
Laurinburg, North Carolina

Coordinating Editor
Anna-Carolyn Stirewalt Gilbo

Consulting Editor
Marsha White Warren

Library of Congress number: 87-061394
ISBN 0-932662-68-4
ISBN 0-932662-71-4 (pbk.)

Acknowledgments

This anthology sponsored by the Friends of Weymouth, Inc.
was funded in part by grants from:

The A.J. Fletcher Foundation,
The North Carolina Arts Council, and
The National Endowment for the Arts

Foreword

My latest Weymouth-inspired poem hot in my hand, I stopped by *The Pilot* to see Sam Ragan. Sam sat behind the mountainous horizontal-file-of-a-desk, and we talked about how everyone who has stayed at Weymouth has been inspired to create a poem, a painting, or a piece of music in its honor. He again talked about the dream he had shared at the Poetry Festival in 1979: to publish an anthology of poetry written by writers who had been at The Weymouth Center. We agreed the time had come; and Sam, with his busy schedule, wanted me to handle the project.

After thinking about the immensity of such an undertaking, I knew it was more than a one-person job, and Marsha Warren was the very one to help. I was pleased when in July of 1986, she agreed to lend her experience to the project. She began the tedious job of writing grants, and together we began collecting information and searching for names and addresses. We read scraps of paper—sometimes with a magnifying glass, the backs of envelopes scratched with barely decipherable names, initialed poems stuffed in folders, even reservations on old calendars. We never found some of the writers even with all our efforts by letter, by phone calls made by a "telephonophobic", and by putting a notice in *The Pilot*.

I was delighted when Sam asked me to write a personal foreword for the book. Weymouth had become very important to me: a place to write, to learn, to be with friends. At Weymouth I have watched my daughter grow into a published poet, my son receive an award for his poem about his grandfather, and I have spent time in-residence with my father, discussing writing and browsing in the library late at night.

The Board of the Friends of Weymouth, the sponsoring group, was enthusiastic from the start, as was Jack Roper and the St. Andrews Press when approached about publishing the book. Poems began to arrive, many with notes telling about the importance of Weymouth to the writers. We began our search for art work, and we want to give a special thank you to the artists for all their help and cooperation. Then, one cold morning in January, Mr. Frank Fletcher called to say we had been granted money from the A.J. Fletcher Foundation. We were half the way there. In June, we were notified we had a grant from the North Carolina Arts Council and the National Endowment for the Arts. We express our sincere gratitude to these organizations.

Many people deserve our appreciation for all their help and encouragement. For permissions to reprint poems, we especially thank Dorothy Owen, Marguerite Stem, Linda Walters, R.B. Daly, and Nancy Boyd Sokoloff, daughter of James Boyd.

This book is a "thank you" from all of us who have had the privilege to be a part of the spirit and mystique of Weymouth.

—Anna-Carolyn Gilbo, Coordinating Editor

Acknowledgments

The Editors are grateful to the following authors and publishers for permission to reprint poems from the works listed below:

Acorn Press for "Haunted" from *North Carolina's 400 Years: Signs Along The Way* by Claire Cooperstein.

America Press for "Beyond The Dream" by Emily Sargent Councilman and "Endangered Specimen" by Helen M. Copeland in *America*.

The Anderson Agency for "Southern Pines Depot" by Jody Scott.

The Arts Journal for "The Lasting" by Paul Jones.

John F. Blair, Publisher for "My Father's Curse" from *The White Stallion* by Guy Owen.

The Carolina Wren Press for "The Rimland" by Cindy Paris from *A Living Culture in Durham*.

Colonnades for "Late Afternoon Thunderstorm in the Carolinas" by Andrew J. Angyal.

Crucible for "Words" by Nancy Frost Rouse.

Emrys Journal for "Staining the Porch Rocker" by Rebecca McClanahan Devet and "Late Snow" by Mary Kratt.

The Glens Fall Review for "The Harbor" by Richard DeLos Mar.

Mid-American Review for "Formal Gardens" by Ann Dunn.

Moore Publishing Company for "On Keeping Abreast of Things" from *A Squadron of Roses* by Calvin Atwood.

Muse for "On A Dove's Wings" by Lei Zimmerman.

McNally and Loftin for "Unofficial Greeter" from *Journey Proud* by Thad Stem, Jr.

Outerbridge and Blue Coot Press, from *Middle Creek Poems*, for "When January Is Cold" by Shelby Stephenson.

Pembroke Magazine for "Verse Letter" by Sister Bernetta Quinn O.S.F. and "Mimosa" by Mary C. Snotherly.

The Pilot for all those poems that have appeared in "Southern Accent."

Quill Books for "Poet" by Gwyn Harris.

St. Andrews Press for "Mahalia Jackson Gets Ready To Go On Stage" from *Strawberry Harvest* by Sally Buckner, "To The Mistress" from *Visualize* by Bobby G. Price, and "Let Us Walk Into April" from *A Walk Into April* by Sam Ragan.

St. Andrews Review for "The Watchman" by Fred Chappell.

Tyndale House Publishers for "The Holiest of Holies" from the novel *Katie* by Margaret A. Graham.

Wind Literary Journal for "The Prey" by Nina A. Wicker.

The Word Works for "How To Leave A Small Town in the Dark," by Shirley G. Cochrane.

Weymouth—A Preface

It was Paul Green as much as anyone who gave voice and support to the early efforts to preserve Weymouth. And that great man of great heart and spirit, with long ties of friendship with James and Katharine Boyd, would be proud of today's Weymouth Center for the Arts and Humanities.

Green himself was the first to pledge $1,000 toward buying the Weymouth estate of the Boyds back from Sandhills Community College. Bob Drummond, a Moore County resident, was the first to contribute $20,000 to the effort and later to add an equal amount to the cause.

The preservation idea itself, however, began with Elizabeth Stevenson (Buffie) Ives of Southern Pines, a longtime friend of Katharine Boyd, and she elicited the support of others to form the Friends of Weymouth.

There were many involved in the early days of the Friends of Weymouth campaign to raise $700,000 to purchase the 215-acre estate. The list would be too long to name, but some of those who contributed time, money and energy were Ray Kotryla, Admiral I.J. Gallantin, Lena Stewart, Veronese Atkins, Capt. Sherman Betts, and others.

The purchase was made and Governor Jim Hunt came down to dedicate the Center. Many of the people in Moore County and across the state shared in the pride of the accomplishment. The Weymouth Center for the Arts and Humanities, dedicated to the creative spirit and the human aspirations for the good life—the dream of Paul Green—was a reality.

Katharine Boyd, who also had that dream and vision for her beloved Weymouth, would have been proud that day, and I think she would be proud today of not only the reality but the concept which has been maintained.

The first program to be initiated at the Weymouth Center was a writers-in-residence plan which had been proposed and endorsed by the Friends of Weymouth. It was a natural development because Weymouth had been a place of hospitality for writers in the early days of the 1920's and 1930's when James Boyd was writing his novels, short stories and poems, and helping to launch, as Jonathan Daniels insisted, the Southern Literary Renaissance. Writer friends of the Boyds such as Thomas Wolfe, F. Scott Fitzgerald, Sherwood Anderson, Maxwell Perkins, Paul Green, Lawrence Stallings, John Galsworthy, and William Faulkner came to visit, and some stayed to write.

There are many stories of lively conversations among these writers who changed and helped shape the American literary landscape of the 20th Century.

The Writers-in-Residence Program was a natural in light of that tradition, and since its beginning in 1979 some 300 writers—at first from North Carolina and now from across the nation—have shared in the creative mystique which is Weymouth.

The first Writer-in-Residence was the talented novelist and poet, the late

Guy Owen. It was a deliberate choice because the genial Guy Owen had been a strong supporter of the establishment of the Weymouth Center. He was joined in that first week of residency by poets Agnes McDonald and Betty Adcock, and they were followed by others of talent, devotion and dedication to writing. The spirit of Weymouth was catching, and some of those who came in the early days have returned to feed upon that spirit and to get the creative juices flowing again.

At the first North Carolina Poetry Festival in 1979 the hope was expressed that at some point in the future an anthology of Weymouth poetry could be published, with the poems of those who had been Writers-in-Residence, or had been leaders in literary programs at the Center, included in the book.

Through the splendid work of Anna-Carolyn Gilbo and Marsha Warren, and the cooperation of Jack Roper and the St. Andrews Press, this hope has become a reality. The Friends of Weymouth are proud to offer these collected poems of 112 poets as a monument to the spirit of Weymouth.

The book, we think, is aptly named—Weymouth.

—*Sam Ragan, Editor*

Contents

James Boyd—*Wedding Anniversary* 3

THE PLACE

Tom Hawkins—*The House of Hounds' Gate* 7
Mae Woods Bell—*Another Weymouth April* 8
Lois Holt—*Respite* 9
Ann Dunn—*Formal Gardens* 10
Shirley Moody—*In the Thick of Night* 11
Ellen Turlington Johnston-Hale—*Summer Night* 12
Margaret Boothe Baddour—*Windows at Weymouth* 13
Irene Dayton—*Storm Over Weymouth* 14
Reed Whittemore—*Narrative* 15
Kate Blackburn—*Overheard at a Wedding: Weymouth* 16
Mary Kratt—*Late Snow* 17
Lorraine M. Hueneke—*Weymouth* 18
Kate Kelly Thomas—*Shelby at Weymouth* 19
Rebecca Ball Rust—*At Weymouth Stables* 20
Shirley Graves Cochrane—*How to Leave a Small Town in the Dark* 21
Sally Svee—*Autumn Morning Reverie* 22
Andrew J. Angyal—*Late Afternoon Thunderstorm in the Carolinas* 23
Marsha White Warren—*Bound North* 25
Cindy Paris—*The Rimland* 26
Mary Belle Campbell—*Weymouth Rhapsodie* 27
Bobby Sidna Hart—*Weymouth Bath* 28
Anne Russell—*The Herb Lady of Weymouth* 29
Lu Overton—*Weymouth Interlude* 30
Maud R. Oaks—*Rooms* 31
Mitchell Forrest Lyman—*Save the Pines* 32
Marie Gilbert—*Tree Felled at the Corner of Bennett and Connecticut* 33
Wilma Loeschen Barefoot—*Breakdown* 34
Calvin Atwood—*On Keeping Abreast of Things* 35
Lee Steuer—*A Party for the N.C. Symphony* 37
Sandra Redding—*Communion* 38

E. Waverly Land—*Up the Watertower, Halfway* 39

Anna-Carolyn Stirewalt Gilbo—*Beneath the Slate Roof* 41

Agnes McDonald—*Breakfast and After at Weymouth* 42

Betty Adcock—*Written at a Country Mansion of the
   1920's, Now Partially Restored as a Retreat for Poets* 43

THE SPIRIT

Gladys Owings Hughes—*So Much Depends* 47

Grace L. Gibson—*In the Best Circles* 48

Emily Herring Wilson—*Splitting Wood* 49

Susan B. Katz—*A Week at Weymouth* 50

Sallie Nixon—*Now We Are One of Them* 51

John Foster West—*A Note to James Boyd—Spring, 1985* 52

Michael McFee—*A Week at Weymouth* 53

Reynolds Price—*Two Poems from a Journal* 55

Elaine L. Goolsby—*Under the Dog Star* 56

Elinor Owens Gray—*Ghosts, Past and Present* 57

Joel Chace—*3 A.M.* 58

Grace Ellis—*Calling Captain* 59

Claire Cooperstein—*Haunted* 60

Barbara Rosson Davis—*Weymouth* 61

Will Blythe—*The Life I've Made* 62

Lisa-Catherine Yost—*TO OPEN my self* 63

Gwyn Harris—*Poet* 64

Gloria T. Delamar—*Weymouth—the Boyds—and the
   Transmigration of Energy* 65

Virginia Love Long—*Summer Nights at Weymouth* 66

Emily Sargent Councilman—*Beyond the Dream* 67

Sam McKay—*The Silent Chase* 69

Margaret A. Graham—*The Holiest of Holies* 70

Rebecca McClanahan Devet—*Staining the Porch Rocker* 71

Hazel Foster Thomas—*The Message* 72

Mary C. Snotherly—*Mimosa* 73

William T. Delamar—*I Cry* 74

Thad Stem, Jr.—*Unofficial Greeter* 75

Anna Wooten-Hawkins—*Students* 76

Lei Zimmerman—*On a Dove's Wings* 77

Paul Jones—*The Lasting* 78
Salvatore Salerno—*A Plate of Bread* 79
Katherine Russell Barnes—*Second Child* 80
Judy Hogan—*Book XI of Light Food* 81
Kathryn Stripling Byer—*Weep-Willow* 82
Nancy Frost Rouse—*Words* 83
Mary Warren-Harris—*Storm Clouds* 84
Constance Pierce—*The Green Woman* 85
Marcia McCredie—*What Dreams? for Bob* 87
Kay Nelson—*Your Scarf* 88
Jean Morgan—*Leni: Letter from Castle Berg* 89
Ardis Messik Hatch—*Years of Time* 90

—AND BEYOND

Sam Ragan—*Let Us Walk Into April* 93
Ronald H. Bayes—*Star With Sun* 94
Heather Ross Miller—*Passport* 95
James Applewhite—*Light Beyond Thought* 96
Sally Buckner—*Mahalia Jackson Gets Ready to Go on Stage* 97
Hilda Downer—*Shadows that Steep in Dreams of the New Ground* 99
Fred Chappell—*The Watchman* 100
Clyde Edgerton—*Outdoors is Closed* 102
Guy Owen—*My Father's Curse* 103
Judith Holmes Settle—*Eyeblink* 104
Julian Long—*Autumn Catalogue* 105
Betty Miller Daly—*Acknowledgement* 107
Grace DiSanto—*Less is More* 108
Bobby G. Price—*To the Mistress* 109
Thomas Walters—*Tape Wrap* 110
R.T. Smith—*Night Anthem in West Negril* 112
Luther Stirewalt—*Cloud Passage* 113
Nina A. Wicker—*The Prey* 114
Harriet Doar—*All I Know About Berries* 115
Julie Suk—*Sitting Out a War Once-Removed* 117
Leon Carrington Hinton—*The Other Side* 118
Charles Fort—*Salieri's Sonnet* 119

Ruth Moose—*In the Old Camden Market on Main Street* 120
Stephen E. Smith—*The Fence* 121
Helen M. Copeland—*Endangered Specimen* 122
Shelby Stephenson—*When January is Cold* 123
Sister Bernetta Quinn, O.S.F.—*Verse Letter* 124
Maureen D Sutton—*High Noon at the Matinee* 125
Richard DeLos Mar—*Harbor* 126
Joanna Allred McKethan—*Sacred Shadows* 127
Stephen Morris Roberts—*October Shadows* 128
Dean M. Hale—*O.R. Mask* 129
Rebecca J. Finch—*Passiflora* 130
Pamolu Oldham—*Cameron '85* 131
Ruby P. Shackleford—*The Drums Come* 132
Ann Deagon—*Claiming the Body* 133

Art Work

Arthur Frank—*Portrait of James Boyd* 2
Danila Devins—*The Weymouth Meet* 4
Danila Devins—*Robert with Wilbur and Sam* 4
Maureen Frederick—*Dogwood Blossoms* 6
Jody Scott—*Southern Pines Depot* 24
Ann Listokin—*Weymouth Ice Gardens* 36
Catharine Callaway Stirewalt—*Original Moore County Hound*......40
Nancy Williams—*Evening Star* 46
Meredith Martens—*Male Fox* 68
Benjamin E. Bessette—*Duck Decoys* 86
Richard Munger Preyer—*Virgin Pines* 92
Susan Carlton Smith—*Don Quixote* 98
Mary B. Preyer—*Iris* 106
Richard Munger Preyer—*Character Study* 116

Weymouth

*to the Boyd Family
and the Spirit of Weymouth*

Portrait of James Boyd   oil

James Boyd

Wedding Anniversary

It sometimes seems as if that snowy day
When, from your house and hill, the flying sleigh
With silver notes bore you and me away,
Were only just last year;
The black trees stand so clear,
So clear the snowy hill, the silver sleigh-bells shine,
So warm your narrow mitten lies in mine.

But when at other times I search my heart
And look upon my life in every part,
I feel that you have known me from the start,
I feel that you have known
Years that I seemed alone,
That in the bounty of your patient love
There are no days of mine it knows not of.

The Weymouth Meet   watercolor

Robert with Wilbur and Sam   pen and pencil

THE PLACE

...in the house of thoughts and spaces

Maureen Frederick

Dogwood Blossoms   batik

Tom Hawkins

The House of Hounds' Gate

Ideas retreat down halls
as doors hold things back;
silent kitchens stand surprised.

I walk this new remembering
that grows more vast at night.
My blind feet pad to particular light,
a small glimmering among the shadow.

In the house of
thoughts and spaces
rooms with windows
and without
open into each other;

staircases proceed up
a scale of height,
and small sets of steps
lift up or let down
two, three at a time.

Visions framed in windows
come near the flower
and are scratched by branches
at the screen,

rooms empty as my brain
where something was, or might be,
or might have been.

Mae Woods Bell

Another Weymouth April

Some years it's dogwood blossoms,
Big as teacups,
Challenging the postcard version.
Some years it's wisteria
Weaving nets
To catch Spring...
This year it's violets.

Violets
Forgetting their traditional status,
To stand daringly tall—and blue—
Blue as the seas off Devon's cliffs
Where violets belong,
Where Drake and Barlow, Amadas and Raleigh,
Looked westward.

Respite

When all else fails,
there is March
to drive us mad.
The wettest one on record.
I am covered with mildew,
saturated to my very soul.
Load my car in a heavy mist.
This is the Piedmont—the foot of the mountain
surely, the Sandhills will have absorbed
the overflow.
I am a sister to the sun
more desperate than most
to feel its rays.
Just south of Sanford
the sun breaks through thinning clouds,
I look for familiar signs—
the road bearing to the left
through "horse country,"
one last turn through the gates
(the hounds at least are there).
From the great house,
comes the sound of applause.
I could make it to the concert,
ease into the ballroom unobserved
but the sky has cleared.
Pollen falls over the garden—a yellow mist
covers my sweater, burns my eyes.
I brush it from my hair.
No one is there to notice.
I kneel beside the pool
to watch the goldfish—
reflecting.

Ann Dunn

Formal Gardens

I.

Nothing can breathe the water lily is white with
pink memory spiked grenade it blooms at the heart
of sprawling consequence comfortable in dead air
life floats on Southern afternoons I want to leap
cover its near explosion with my belly save
the world from its beauty become a fountain any
act to break to make the willow move

II.

Frog squats on peripheral leaf of giant lily
snatches at bugs with head only skilled dancer I
move frog skin cracks through the top of its
other atmosphere goldfish I didn't see before
motion slides back into its shadow later
frog is back and I know how to be still until
there is something to move for

III.

Where you were concentric ridges smooth to glass
so fast I can't finish thought olive to chartreuse
the pond says I am final mystery and no surprises
here I ask the flat eye my only question drink
the underside of lilies and the sky even water
bugs get yanked through the mirror by the red
flash of fish surprise speed this side is no
match for hunger underneath the tough old crepe
drops another season purple fists hit the water
with a sigh I too will leave an echo where
I lived

Shirley Moody

In the Thick of Night

Darkness cannot separate into parts
as light into colors.
Darkness is an unbroken whole
and heavy container.

After being with great light,
I re-enter darkness
and cannot see where to go,
so I remain
listening where I cannot hide
from finding myself.

And like any moon gathers whatever light
can be found, wicking whatever is leftover
in this darkness,
I give it all back like an afterimage.

And though I change, I remain
a moonchild,
constant and powerless,
compact and the same,
pearl-small and so alone
in this velvet denseness of night.

Ellen Turlington Johnston-Hale

Summer Night

When sleep won't come,
sit outside on terrace stoop,
hear the tree frogs
sing midnight cacophonies,
accompanied by cricket chorus
and soft percussions—
willows sweeping,
rustled by a restless wind.

When sleep won't come,
walk around this sprawling house
on gentle paths
and watch a radiant half-moon
climbing, climbing slowly up
through the branches of a pine
to the top, then pulling free
like some glowing, graceful dove.

When sleep won't come,
find a place by pillared porch,
listen, then, for the ghosts
of Thomas Wolfe, Paul Green, the ones
who walked by night when sleep came hard,
and watched this moon,
this Weymouth moon.

Margaret Boothe Baddour

Windows at Weymouth

A white rose flakes where it crept to bloom
inside on the window sill in a dark hall.
Far away—orange blossoms—sweet on the air.

Glass ripples, waves over the eighty-one
latticed places that enclose us, the arches,
bays, rectangles we look in, look out of....

Gothic panes reveal lavender, twin iris the color
of eyes. Yellow roses drape the old brick wall,
the stuccoed pool room, the pebbled lotus pond.

We want to be close to the iris, lavender tufted,
yellow throats—to think those paper-thin folds
enclose the ruffles, veins, fuzz of the full-blown ones.

Cherry trees, bowing in rows, grace the lawn
like skirts, like picture hats. A man named Green
keeps pushing back the forest, holding the woods.

In the holly tree a frantic brown cardinal
guards her rusted eggs. Red lover, green worm
painted against the pines—and the dogwood dying.

Eighty-one places frame this and that—
the silver-haired one on the veranda, the one
typing in the garden. The ones we only know about

from sweaters left in closets, notes in mirrors,
saw in these sashed casements—shuttered, shuddered.
And we want to picture things as if seen

through windows. Two women sit on bricks
in sunlight, and it's terrible looking through
these windows at people crying....

Glass waves, ripples over eighty-one arched,
bayed, sashed, splayed, latticed places where we
look in, look out. We enclose them.

Irene Dayton

Storm Over Weymouth

In this historic house of Weymouth, thunder
vibrates from all directions
ricochets among the pines.
Working on poems with a friend
we see lightning careen from the sky
the splitting and splintering
of the sun in the night.
In thunderstorms, I remember, my mother
often carried a feather pillow.

After storm rides over
we open doors, return to our poems.
Cool air floods in with call of the cicadas.
Frogs marshal quavering voices
They are blooming in the garden
They are blooming in the night
Cicadas and frogs waken the dark.
Their rhythms like cadences of poems
we may not achieve.
Our sleep is attuned to their throbbing.

At morning light by wing of the house
we find a loblolly pine
slashed and ringed with gashes
the ground fragmented with bark.
I peel off the wet cambium pieces
and wring them like leather.
The day, as before,
endures the hot, dry winds of summer
and tremors a rhythmical phrase.
The sun is as ever,
but we know the sun splintered in the night.

Narrative

What I am telling you now
moves and must always be moving
                              so that
if it is in the kitchen it must be drifting
out into the hall and up the long stair as
far perhaps as the attic where it must
float out toward the mountain where a fine lady
perhaps is waiting

Yes what I am telling you now is climbing the steep side
                              and
an hour perhaps will do it
to the top where the lady is waiting

For why would I tell you that which I tell you
were there not always this movement
                              this
drifting out from the attic unto the mountain
and up the steep side
                              for
were there not always this movement you would be bored
and drumming the kitchen table
                              but
because you are hearing this drifting you are now listening
waiting

Kate Blackburn

Overheard at a Wedding: Weymouth

Ordinarily his words would not rise, being leaden
but on this wedding day there is weightlessness:
champagne, balloons, the trill of wine-soaked laughter
the sum of all the suns of all May brides ever
distilled like cognac, bright & crisp as mint.

But the German bartender is serious today.
He will have the college kid turn the greasy ball
of the Third Reich over again & again
while they snap the beer tins & pop champagne
dispense scotch, & scotch with a splash, & scotch with a twist.
His voice urges: *Wrestle the deep Jew;*
run east of every place you've ever been.
"Laura" melts from the ballroom; a snare thumps like a cardboard box.

In the corner room unscreened I type;
the machine murmurs continuo to the glitter of laughter;
the guttural immediacy of the closest voice.
The German hails independent political conscience—
the greasy ball is string soaked in my own fat.
I am a voyeur with thin skin.

A winter poem is making itself out of this May day
Oriental, tightly wrought, gossamer—a landscape
etched cold with old fear and forgotten.

I am like the German: Dachau prisoner of what I've read
and dreamed. We, two, alone at this wedding
still hunt for the lost who chant in the marsh
listen for the lost who pray in the wet wood.
This fear we have wilts and must be hurriedly tossed
like a bridal bouquet.

Mary Kratt

Late Snow

But why
when it came,
snow all day,
did the full-flowering trees,
those April fools,
catch most of it,
bend
and break,
the more in bloom
the more severe the damage,
lost,
gone,
given away.

Lorraine M. Hueneke

Weymouth

Softly,
a scent of pine
needles the Georgian house,
while wisps of words roam the hallways
and wait.

Kate Kelly Thomas

Shelby at Weymouth

Eyes flash
fingers run through red hair
a quick grin covers his candid face.

He leads listeners from high-ceilinged rooms
across pine-needled lawns
away from tall houses and concrete.
We follow him
to a loamy tobacco farm
and he's in the middle of his poem.
With Spring in his face
he relives the life...
pulls yellow lugs, waters sweaty mules
at noon, strums his guitar at sundown,
as drying leaves whiff the air.

With eyes closed
he runs again the path to the creek
hooks the cat-fish
hears his line sing...lands him!
    A barefoot boy with cool
    green moss between his toes.

Rebecca Ball Rust

At Weymouth Stables

Under the eye
of the black iron rider
on the black iron horse atop the cupola,
past the bright new padlock
on the tack room door,
over the jagged, splintered sill
and in through the open window
                                I climb
around the shards of broken glass
and onto the cracked cement.

Empty now the stalls, and quiet,
their earthen floors criss-crossed
in the patterns of old rake marks.
The corner stall, its hard earth rounded
in three uneven hollows,
breathes the presence of the old stallion,
who lay and listened, lay and finally
found his recognizable truths
in the blue yell of sky
and green scream of pine
                                beyond.

Shirley Graves Cochrane

How to Leave a Small Town in the Dark

The train is the best way to go
even though it leaves at six a.m.
You can walk to the station—
again, the best way. Move
through patches of dark
into patches of light.

Those shapes that loom close
to the fence are horses.
In daylight they turn away
when you speak. In dark
they protect you. And then
you step into light.
The next dark spot
is straight road
until you get to town.

At least once, a dark figure
may come toward you
but he will say
Good morning, reminding you
this is not night. What harm
can befall you in a place
where the railroad track runs
through the middle of town?

You are safe—see ahead
the depot lights. Inside,
the benches of childhood
await you. Sit quietly—
wait for the train whistle
that has shaped
your morning dreams.

Sally Svee

Autumn Morning Reverie

This sun dapples a pattern
  through thinning leaves,
    and lights the edges of the breeze.

That sun warmed my fingers and face,
  and made lazy promises.

This sun turns green to gold,
  and gold to brown.

That sun woke sleeping buds
  into riots of color,
    and made all things possible.

This sun reminds me of the date,
  and tells me to hurry.

That sun smiled encouragement,
  and said to take my time.

This sun hides,
  then peers out to caution me
    to burrow into a quiet cocoon
      and wait again for

—that sun.

Andrew J. Angyal

Late Afternoon Thunderstorm in the Carolinas

What cosmic vandalism
toppled those two
venerable white oaks,
shaking the dead
from their sleep,
toppling slate roofs
on their chalky heads,
leaving only a grey
squirrel to run
chattering along
the fallen trunks
while the cross
on the steeple
tilts askew
against the afternoon sky?

Jody Scott

Southern Pines Depot   photo illustration

Marsha White Warren

Bound North

The Silver Star
echoes its way north
through Southern Pines
each morning at 7:56
glides down the main street
past horse farms
virgin pines
pecan groves
moans through the same state
where bloodhounds once
sniffed slaves
down from trees
out of hay wagons and barns
before they could get
underground.

The Rimland

In the resinous forest
a thin snake,
a strip of braided beauty,
threads its way,
black on brown,
through the pine needles.
Where the path breaks
blackberry bushes,
muscadine vines
grow tangled.
This pasture is rinsed
in sunlight.
Every blade stands
separate.
A woodpecker
sets off a thrumming
steady and insistent
as the heart.
How thin, I think,
the membrane between
despair and joy.

Mary Belle Campbell

Weymouth Rhapsodie

Debussy's turn-of-the-century
concert piece,
the autumn garden,
Monet's shadowy Morning Mist,
a thunderstorm gathering—
liquid fragments of melody
crash like sheets of glass,
intermittent sunlight
intruding, irridescent
splashes bouncing
off a dappled fountain bowl
filled with light.

Late afternoon concert,
sunrays slanting across the lawn,
low to the horizon,
transform November pine-needle
greens and browns to gold.
Two pre-teen riders, velvet helmeted,
walk their horses across the meadow,
girls, and horses, too,
deep in conversation, unknowingly
involved in the rhapsodie.

Bobby Sidna Hart

Weymouth Bath

It's old-timey.
Let the brown water run
Until clear.

No shower here.
Take a quart kitchen pot
For rinsing.

The water's hot.
Four quarts rinse the soapsuds,
Two the sand.

Shiver and stand.
Put your clothes on faster
Than you planned.

Anne Russell

The Herb Lady of Weymouth

She dug her bony fingers into winterhard earth
I'll plant alyssum here, she said
And there I'll plant some marigolds
You can't see it, but beneath these weeds
There's a garden waiting to be reborn
I'll put a border of bricks around it
You won't recognize this place next spring
I'm just an old woman who lives alone
Not much good to anyone
But I love to make things grow.

Lu Overton

Weymouth Interlude

A train croons in the night—
not far, not near,
a cricket's at the door,
hounds bark not far away.
Cool air sweeps through screens
    of hallways, rooms, and doors.
No other sounds intrude.

A pauper may be king where pine trees rule
and Weymouth lends the grace in house and land.
No hours here demand attention to a chore,
no classes to attend nor meetings chair.

Time's segments do not interrupt
    a train of thought:
night and day—morning, evening, afternoon—
    any could be now.
One continuous flow of time, marked only
    by arrive and leave,
is before me here. There is a feeling
of limitlessness of time
    in large, but limited, space.

Where time flow is so strong, space limits
    seem unreal.

I shall move in and out for six brief days—
    and spend a lifetime
in futile attempts
to regain
the Weymouth experience.

Maud R. Oaks

Rooms

"My room" at Weymouth
  Overlooks a garden
Of herbs and iris
  Where partridges bob and bow
Along the paths
  Like buxom ladies in a courtly dance,
Where trees have doors
  Which open only at the touch
Of gnomes at night,
  And where quite mortal poets
Sit among the blooms
  And pen immortal verse
In rainbow hues.

Whatever else shall be
  "My room"
Among the promised "many"
  In my next abode,
I hope one window will look out
  Upon a garden
Where "bob whites" bow and bob,
  Where gnomes have homes,
Where poets sit 'mid prismed light
  And sing about the cosmos
In one flower.

Mitchell Forrest Lyman

Save the Pines

I dwell among the oaks, which at this meridian
    go bare, beginning in late August,
    making a clutter in the walkways
    until the last dead leaf is ejected
    by spring green.

I rue the loss of pines to the pine bark beetle....
    It has some obscure Latin name, of course,
    but by whatever name, it kills;
    its guerrilla army invades under cover of bark,
    and chokes off the food supply.

By the time I'm aware that something's amiss,
    the tree is dying,
    and the beetles have moved on to another victim,
    unheard, unseen, except by birds,
    of whom there are not enough to combat the menace.

Yes, I rue the loss of pines
    for I am living as best I can
    in The Pine State,
    where the long leaves, needles, tags, or trash
    descend as noiselessly as the beetles,
    throughout the year,
    but always in balance
    so that the image is forever green,
    and growing.

Marie Gilbert

Tree Felled at the Corner of Bennett and Connecticut

It was at least a yard and a half in diameter,
level to the ground as power saws could make it.
The remains of the giant oak, fresh cut, live white,
smelled of wood working shops and of lumber yards.
More than that, it smelled of hurricane Hazel
breaking the drought, of twelve inch snow
setting a record, coming like white magic
to show folks how to stop, of the house
across the street burning in the night
sending occupants next door for shelter.
It smelled of cool shade, lemonade, swings
sang with the wind and with wrens. Somewhere
in a labyrinth of branches, the homeplace
of generations of squirrels clung weathered.
Now level to the ground, a stepping stone to nowhere
while the fresh cut sweet mash smell still lingers
we'll read history in the air.
When the new white cut fades to earth shade
we'll read it noble as a grave ledger.

Wilma Loeschen Barefoot

Breakdown

Like a gyro
in a cage of
brittle bones
the thought
chases itself
around, I want
to go outside
outside, outside.

The long windows look
upon a field of chopped
corn stalks holding
fall plowed earth down.
Little cars hurry on the
highway, the scene could
use a splash of red, a
cardinal on the wing. A
flare of light on the
hearth would be welcome.

Icicles in the arteries of
the mind begin to melt, a
slow trickle of thaw. I heard
shots awhile ago. Someone wants
to stop the motion of living
things and I am not ready to
be mistaken for a bird in flight.
I could take a walk if only I
could take the safety of the
walls with me.

I think you think my thoughts
but, I am unable to think yours.
Will you miss me if I go out
into the glare of sunlight or
just one day realize that the
silence has taken
a different tone?

Calvin Atwood

On Keeping Abreast of Things

Now that is seems like Spring
keep me a breast
tell me where the flowers are
when the willows bend
keep me in lavender
keep telling me
there's room for me
in places where the red bud blooms.

I need to cancel
doom and blood,
need to know
where blossoms break,
when Spring blows home again,
I want to see earth
crack wide as your eyes
when love arrests.

So keep in touch
keep touching me
and most of all:

keep me a breast.

Ann Listokin

Weymouth Ice Gardens   for piano and violin

Lee Steuer

A Party for the N.C. Symphony
(For Rose Barlow)

After the last long note,
the musicians move through the pines
no less musically than the symphony,
the concerto, the quartet.
I sit sewing threads of my heart,
hoping they'll hold, not tear.
The performers laugh, a little giddy
with wine, the harvest moon, a place to play.
They touch off chords of another music.
My heartstrings quiver
with threads and shards of thought,
difficult to manage,
easy to lose.

Sandra Redding

Communion

For most of my life
on such weighty matters
as God or No-God
I've remained a fence-sitter.

But last October
while walking
the pine-needle paths
of Weymouth
an intoxicating scent
lured me to purple miracles.

Kneeling there
I sampled one, then another
proclaimed the muscadine *divine*.

E. *Waverly Land*

Up the Watertower, Halfway

Tuesday I decided I was fearless
and to prove it I climbed up the watertower
halfway.
No one was around when I crossed the field full of sand spurs and
climbed over the barbed wire fence.
A sunny fall afternoon, I should be able to see quite far.
I promised myself secret rewards for climbing past my fear.
Reaching to hold the ladder, which began ten feet from the
ground, I said this is easy.
But a third of the way up I began my old refrain—
What if I fall?
I tightened my hold and went two more rungs.
I tightened my hold even more, so tight I could go no further.
Looking around, but not at the ground, I congratulated myself
for climbing higher than ever before.
Going all the way to the top just to prove it to me was silly.
Why not not do it, but say I did? Only I would know I did only
half. No one was around to encourage me, no one was around
to look good for, so while still looking up, I climbed down.

And now I think that if all the climbing I did—
up halfway and down halfway—had all been up,
I'd be on top of that watertower still.
If I were
I hope you'd have missed me by now.

Original Moore County Hound   pencil

Anna-Carolyn Stirewalt Gilbo

Beneath the Slate Roof

At night
I close my eyes
and see
the hounds of stone
leap down
desert their posts.
They chase
through virgin pines
to bay at shadows
in the fields
while in my room
beneath the slate
I summon Wolfe, Fitzgerald, Boyd
and all the spirits
of the house:
   Come, touch
    my dark,
      my waiting pen.

Agnes McDonald

Breakfast and After at Weymouth

On a day of rain and roses
that throb like pulses
among grackles and thrushes,
through the glass of doorfans
like breeze-blown pools, I watch
pines scatter yarrow
and hawkweed, pennycress
and shepherd's purse, to where
mirages of mist and meadow
joust, curtsey, dance reels,
raise tents for shows. As a child
all people of earth filed past me,
Breugel faces staring at every turn.

We are each performers in the next year's play
a scrap of red
a hand waving
a tune for a crude madrigal.

Betty Adcock

Written at a Country Mansion of the 1920's, Now Partially Restored as a Retreat for Poets

Our shoes clamor in empty chambers,
room after room, and the sunlight's
whole animal is asleep on bare floors.
Beyond the undraped windows, gardens crouch
deranged beneath their wild invaders.
Only the high pines and the willows
have kept to their places under the sky.
The vast hollows of the house whine, beginning
to know they will be filled.

It is impossible not to imagine the past here,
its cliches of pleasure: how the articulate
guests dropped their shoes on Aubussons
in the quiet hour, dressing for dinner,
those evenings that arrived in their best,
their ice-clear stars.
Horses sighed in the stables,
water in the pool, flame on the candles.

As if things were simple.

For you who raised this house, I cast
a time more yellow with summer than ours,
an ease even you could not have known you owned.
And I give you power's inevitable daydream:
a pause, say, after luncheon when murmurs
of servants had diminished, when the guests
had gone each to his right train.
You are gazing at a wedge of sun
breaking on a polished table-edge
when it comes, the sudden bad moment,
and you think of your heart as the air
races with invisible wheels, a feeling like war
or worse, in a flood of unfurnishing light.
Might the word *thieves* have drifted on your lips,
some wish to refurbish the locks, a whisper
directed to no one?

In that moment before you blinked away
erasure, before you woke wholly to the afternoon's
cut flowers, the mirrors, the folded headlines
from Europe, a hand across your eyes—
you might have guessed, almost,
the longleaf pines around this house the last
of their thousand mile forest,
the light changed into *future*, the workings of light
become knowledge toward holocaust.
You might have seen us, strangers flickering
dark here, darker. And the whippoorwill
practicing a dying art.

THE SPIRIT

...only the weave of wind and word

Nancy Williams

Evening Star   watercolor

Gladys Owings Hughes

So Much Depends

After it leaves the pines
tonight the wind holds
its swishing sigh
reaches eaves
and windows of Weymouth.
Now and then our owl
is answered
by artillery that shakes
old timbers,   shatters
bits of poems.

Windsong, bird of prey, mock
war— a descant trio pulls
against silken twitch of words
blindstitch in fleeting grasp.

Owl deftly lifts his small
catch,   soldiers are ferried
toward sleep.   Now
only the weave of wind and word.

Grace L. Gibson

In the Best Circles

Dappled morning light, surf sound stirred
in pines, a mourning dove's insistent call,
boys' faces looking from their frames
into 1932, a window
shade-pull shadow's perfect round swayed
along the polished, wide-board floor: Weymouth
encircles the pregnant past, welcomes the future.

Globes of marigolds mound along the walkways,
old boxwoods scent the patterned garden angles
where old-fashioned herbs are newly planted:
rue (with which "our hearts are laden"), hyssop
for our bruises, lemon thyme, and lavender.

The Boyd family's hospitality,
spread in widening circles of friends who loved
the weather of this place: boys and horses,
roses, acres of virgin pines, good food
and talk of books to weave the canon round.

Now their heirs, no blood kin, descend
past staircase fanlights, open French
doors from library and dining room, new guests
visiting the past, spreading circles of friends.

Emily Herring Wilson

Splitting Wood

The wedge centers on the wood.
The hammer lifts back high
against a November morning:
then he brings it down
as if the hammer knows.

I hear the echo
and move to the window
to watch another work:
the log I couldn't roll
splits evenly. Next year,
it will flame out of
a cold beauty.

Returning to my work, I lift
a delicate page, looking
for the center and
a place to mark it. My heart beats
as rapidly as any woodsman's:
my hands grow stronger,
and my face is hot.

Susan B. Katz

A Week at Weymouth

Funny,
I had thought this place
to be a retreat
silent
the only sounds
perhaps that of
magnolias dripping,
or longleaf pines
letting loose their needles.
What I hadn't counted on
was the nightly clacking,
the ghost of Jim Boyd
alive at the typewriter.
And furthermore
ducking the downright regular
hailstorm:
poems falling from the sky.

Sallie Nixon

Now We Are
One of Them

Along so many wooden ways they move—
through halls and doors, up stairs and down—
all those minds in the monastic night.

A cough,
a sigh,
paper crumpling—
and then the day, left to us.

To awaken here is the thing:
A buzz breeze wafts upward
a morning call of pines,

naming us,
one by one, now
of Weymouth.

John Foster West

A Note to James Boyd—Spring, 1985

Mohawk drums long ago fell silent,
as have you, too, my good unseen host.
I half think that if I suddenly turn,
I will see your fleeting shadow on a wall
or hear your sibilant whisper of greeting
on the vernal breeze that wafts a window curtain
like the white locks of a patriarch, at home.
    Today, I addressed the gold crocus,
early scout clearing the way
for the tribe of blooms that will come after,
when Carolina April occupies your lawn.
And I leaned, to glimpse my likeness, in your pond
and saw a man older than I knew,
as though you might have looked
across my shoulder; when I whirled
no ghost was there, only your huge house
where you lived in peace so many years.
    When I paced the bridle paths
among the quiet pines, head cocked
like an alert squirrel on guard, I fantasized
I heard the swish of footsteps close behind,
companion to my peaceful walk.
But I was daydreaming; caught up
in the sweet security of early spring,
I knew I was alone with deep joy
that I could embrace this brooding place
with affection for the setting and the past
and for you, my most hospitable host.
Permit me to thank you, Sir, for all this:
for your kind consideration in leaving
your world for others to enjoy,
and for having even me, across the years,
as your most appreciative guest, today.

Michael McFee

A Week at Weymouth

1.

I carry my Royal over the threshold,
lay it on the spread bed, say,
Be fruitful and multiply.

2.

Faced with a single outlet,
which would Chekhov choose:
music, light, or the word?

3.

PLEASE DO NOT SNEAK POEMS INTO ROOMS
AS THEY TEND TO ATTRACT VERMIN.

4.

A venerable abbot in a bowtie
comes to me in a dream, and says,

"You may walk in the walled garden
and crush one herb on each finger—
but please, pluck no fruits or flowers.

Birds will minister to you in your cell,
bring fresh gossip and weather reports.
They are such perfect barometers!"

5.

Double shifts at the blank desk
cancelled with caffeine,
phases of a dark moon.

I harvest fatigue like a tenant—
backstrain, grotesque tics,
hand cramps, fingers barely able
to grip another stalk or leaf.

6.

I can't sleep so I count bombs
exploding in pillows of sand
at the nearby camp, a drumbeat
ruthless as the heart in my ear.

7.

Driving out, the days align:
legal sheet and longleaf pine.

Two Poems from a Journal

Praise

This stands for praise—
A book of days
Of frozen terror,
Scalded nights,
The horn of healing,
Tethered flights
To follow that
Tall muffled light:
Whatever name
It wills to bear.

Again

Praise?—this mountain bursting my back,
Blundering out toward day and light
Through me, the space I've fought to hold—
Clear of pain, secure for rest:
One evening glide toward tranquil night?

Pain. Labor. The birth-throes of death—
Mine, for me. Selected by what
Or whom? Sent why?

The source and socket
Of end and start.

What else? *Praise.*

Elaine L. Goolsby

Under the Dog Star

Weymouth hounds roam at night,
leap down from their pedestals
with a dancer's grace. I sit
in the great room and watch
them frolic like puppies on
the sculptured lawn. They circle
the pool, startling the frogs,
drink water with greedy gulps.
With muzzles dripping, they mark
the boundary between yard
and deep wood. I hear them
pant as they trot by.
In that still moment before dawn,
before birds rustle and chirp,
they settle into formal posture
on the pedestals and
wait for the day.

Elinor Owens Gray

Ghosts, Past and Present

She stands in shadow near the stables
witnessing nocturnal rituals—

Two gatepost hounds cat-leap to ground,
stalk woods, gardens, pool, hypnotize
hapless stone creatures caught between them,
sniff out secrets as hounds are born to do.

Horses, manes and tails stretched straight
by the wind, kick up sand along the drive
with coltish hooves. Tiring, they seek
their stalls, munching, crunching,
stomping, settling down.

Hounds nuzzle stall to stall,
back away, hackles rising
and, stone eyes iced with tears,
return to guard duty.

She is free, now, to roam the house.
Entering the usual way she hovers above
the silent piano; fingers lightly travel keys,
brush walls, touch cherished trophies.
Riffling pages she drops a book called DRUMS....

In a lighted room above the kitchen
where servants once slept, typing ceases;
a writer, heart-in-mouth, tilts his head,
listens, shrugs wry shoulders,
resumes tapping out a fantasy:

> She watches ten blooded horses,
> manes and tails flying in the wind,
> clip-clop hollow hooves in concert
> with echoes of baying and whinnying
> in empty stables....

3 A.M.

Gliding around a
curve, my life—
that looms out with the car's
lean and pull—does not
swing back
plumb, but floats just
outside my seated self. I
hover, fluttering
against lives
and landscapes.

This August night's
star-pricked blue dissolves
all but the starkest
distinctions of day. Thrown against
hillsides, pockets of
lights mirror the wide
sky. Outlines of closer
towns, horses, silos, pines
are too
fine. The blue
unity is all. With
a distant blue belief
I make
my way, lulled
by plats and specks of
insects breaking
on the windshield.

Calling Captain

Captain. Here, Captain. Come here, suh.
You seen a hound dog with a tan patch
Just here on his left eye?
One of Mr. Jim Boyd's favorite hounds. Run off this morning.
If Mr. Jim was home now, this thing never would have happened.
He can take all forty of those dogs,
Take them walking right down the middle of Broad Street.
One strays the least little bit,
All he has to do is call that dog by name,
It steps right back in line, pretty as you please.

You. Captain. I ain't got time to fool with you.
Somebody's got to get back there and start cooking.
Those big-time writers sure can eat.
Course, Mr. Anderson, he's not much trouble.
Spends most of his time at the tracks with the horses, you know.
But that Mr. Wolfe.
I've never seen a man could talk so.
Supper be turning stone cold on his plate,
And still he's going on,
Words just pouring out his mouth
Like water out a spout.

Oh, there's always a big commotion up at the house.
Miz Katharine and her workmen.
Knocking down walls, adding a bathroom, making a hall.
And Mr. Jim Boyd kicks up a monstrous ruckus every morning when
      he writes.
Course, it's his secretary who puts down the words.
She's pretty quiet most likely.
But Mr. Jim, he starts at one end of that long study
And walks to the other,
Back and forth, back and forth,
Dictating all the time, you know—
And he wears his hunting boots!

You. Captain. Get over here, suh.
How come you to act such a way?

Claire Cooperstein

Haunted

The birds that sing the morning in recall
the days, the nights, slow motion dawn to dawn.
This manor, framed by undulating lawn,
by sculptured hedges, iris marching tall,
once knew a time unhurried, sweet and slow.
The house is haunted by the long ago.

The terraces still wait for tea and scones.
The library still holds a ghostly trace
of brandy and cigars. The fireplace
hides ghosts of pine logs in its blackened stones.
The Great Room's polished parquet floors recall
the monthly musicales, the Annual Ball.

Upstairs the ghosts of laughing children hide.
So many stairs! I count three flights in all—
two narrow ones, the stairs in the front hall
are wide and gracious, perfect for a bride.
When French doors let the Jasmine breezes in,
the chandeliers start chiming Lohengrin.

The servants' wing is empty now. To reach
the narrow rooms, you go up narrow stairs,
down narrow halls, to find two chairs,
a single bed, one chest of drawers in each.
The kitchen bells keep calling down below:

> *"acres of lawn to mow*
> > *trees to prune, hedges to trim*
> *sterling to polish and put away*
> > *ten beds to make*
> *eight baths to clean*
> > *the dining room seats twelve*
> *the Great Room, thirty-five*
> > *—eighty, if buffet..."*

The ghosts of bells keep ringing down below
—summoning, summoning. Hurry, hurry ...go!

Barbara Rosson Davis

Weymouth

We have left traces of ourselves
in the old house, a strand of hair,
a finger nail on the tile,
scent of jasmine oil in the striped room
where I would give you dawn in the Sandhills—
movement of light leaping the pines,
my pen sparking stars.
I write myself into the desk by the window,
overlook the boxwood maze and fragrant herbs below.

What faces have gazed into the hidden mirror
in the top bureau drawer? I tweeze my brows
and wonder at my heroine—should she tweeze hers?
I am the hunter now, finding bones
of the past hidden in the sounds
of drawers gliding, chairs sliding at a banquet set
in photographs that hang in the hall of Weymouth.
The study is filling up with past lives of poets
who have left their skins behind, their books,
like wild animals leave traces of themselves.

Here the woods swell with words,
the notes of September birds; October's
spice-brown leaves like gloves,
catch falling needles from a crisper air.
It is a place washed clean
by a week full of rain.
Now the marigolds hold light,
the lily-pads dazzle the frog.
Sun brings old shadows into play
as the house widens with the day.

I pursue the ghosts, with intent to converse
one night, only to find feathers flying
and the folding flight of a moth.
By rights I am just a visitor here,
a trace of what has been,
come to Weymouth for the path within.

Will Blythe

The Life I've Made

The sound of silverware
Being sorted floats
Through the spring air
Like one of those past lives
I never led:
Such grace!
And I am up here in my room
Practicing the languages
Of the silent, no notion
Of what to say to anyone.
Tonight they're calling
For soft breezes, moon,
A shower of meteors,
Enough air to clatter
The blinds like bones
As I lie in the dark
Of the life I've made.

Lisa-Catherine Yost

TO OPEN my self
on paper,
I pull me
into a closed ball,
tangle arms
around warm knees,
and only then
unfold my mind
into poetry.

Gwyn Harris

Poet
(Procrastinator or masochist?)

Tiny needles sting
Inside my head
As I drive my day onward—
A sandspur catching
In tender folded velvet,
Relentless captive,
Finally victorious,
Plucked painfully,
Freed in verse.

Gloria T. Delamar

Weymouth—the Boyds—and the Transmigration of Energy

Ghosts inspire the writer's muse
As James types a staccato tune
And Katharine hums her melody.

Like the prickly cones of the long-leaf pine,
The seeds of the mind expand with new births,
And creative surges feed the soul.

Fresh words sing from the spirit
To form realities shaped in black and white,
While the writer forges the chain of continuity.

Summer Nights at Weymouth
(For Sam Ragan)

Silence sings along cool darkened halls.
The house begins to speak: popping floorboards
Creak beneath bare feet. Sometimes an elusive word
Breaks barriers of distant years, snapping death's shackles
In the next room—a snatch of lost melody,
Fragmented sentences still unfinished,
The whisper of prayers cut short.
Here night is a woman wearing moonlight.
Her skirts drag over the terrace,
Gleam through the iris beds. The trailing hem
Threads through the boxwoods, rustling
Over each twisting path. Life is like this:
A garden maze we, pondering, wandering, puzzle out,
Quilting together unexpected turns,
Curves sudden and sharp as the new moon's horns.
Some gnostics insist it does not matter
Which road we choose, if we journey its full length,
Allow our hearts to guide, let hearts
Be nests and love another road we follow out
With faithful feet. We travel sometimes together
And mostly alone, grateful that every road
Brings us back to the garden where startled nightbirds
Break the cathedral hush with drowsy half-notes.
I go inside, mount the stairs slowly.
The moon left her billowing gown behind
Draped over the bannister railing,
Dropped in drifts of luminous haste on the bed's footboard.
Sleep washes in warm rich waves of gladness
Discovering darkness is me, a dreaming woman
Naked and flowering in the summer night.

Emily Sargent Councilman

Beyond the Dream

You and I riding an updraft,
soaring on outstretched wings,
moving in perfect symmetry
to the sound of silence—no
end and no beginning,
no take-off or landing
with awkward wings, unsteady
feet—only an outflowing
past known horizons, powered by
crystal light from eyes
meeting and holding course
together, till time again
is before, and silence after.

Effortless the parting—as if
overtones once heard
would sound for ever.

Meredith Martens

Male Fox   acrylic

Sam McKay

The Silent Chase

Quiet are the hounds of Weymouth.
Calmly they watch the people enter.
Promptly they catch the scent of a novice
and the chase begins. It's a strange pursuit,
not the noisy tracking of one who runs,
nor yet the busy sniffing of trails to find
one freshly made by likely game.
This prey is unaware of the hounds
that follow like soft shadows,
secretly spreading a spell
that charms the heart
among tall trees, trim shrubs,
bewitching flowers radiating light,
and fellowship of kindred minds,
past and present, who gather in these
spacious halls to share their muses.
Lithe with life, the hounds of Weymouth stalk
their victims over field and thicket:
they nudge, tug and draw them back
to the place they guard.

Margaret A. Graham

The Holiest of Holies

Scales removed,
    the light sears.
The holiest of holies
    is truth.

Myths told over and over,
    believed:
Savored morsels
    nourishing the sinew of the will,
The dark side of Shekinah
    cloaking reality—
    admired as love in all its blindness.

Myths must die.
Close the lid on them.
Hush their voices echoing in the hollows
    of your mind;
Lower them gently into the grave
    as lies of love.

Light's pain is not relieved
    through glasses smoked by would-be truth;
Stare light in the face.
It will never die,
Never go away,
But neither will it blind.

Staining the Porch Rocker

I would have left it as it was.
Pale, newly shaven.
Nails poking their heads
through the innocent pine.
The sun would have bleached it
to buckling, the rains
softened it to destruction,
a sweet rotting where ants
and termites make their home.
I have always been one
to love a natural aging.

But you left too soon.
And alone that night
I found a dozen reasons.
My hands were bare.
The stain oily, thick.
I stroked the arms, empty, curved.
The hard back, the slats
driven fast together.
Even the spaces beneath,
the spaces no one sees,
I rubbed,
my hands on the bare wood
darkening.

Hazel Foster Thomas

The Message

Did his face light up
when you called my name
and did he send any word?

Did he mention our hill?
Though it's glazed with snow,
he'll remember springtime,
grasses greening, white orchards.

Tell him the willow
by the pond is greening
and the white swan
is back with his mate.

Tell him the mare
is still afoot
and the soil needs turning.

The boy, should he ask
is an inch taller.
Should he hint of home,
you'll know what to say—
the boy misses him.

Mary C. Snotherly

Mimosa

When I was born, my father planted
a mimosa sapling—to grow with me,
for me to climb when I was ten.
I climbed those limbs—was Tarzan, Jane,
sometimes Boy—and where two branches bent,
I hid a tin, a Prince Albert tobacco box.
Inside, a ruby ring, the prize from Cracker Jacks,
one bluejay feather, silver-tipped and thin,
two glass marbles bright as suns,
a yellow satin ribbon. I'd skin-the-cat,
swing the low limb upside-down—my hair tumbling,
sweeping the ground. Once I climbed so high,
my father came all that way from his office—
home, to bring me down.

Summer nights, when dishes rattled in the sink
and windows lit, and planes and fireflies came
to speckle skies—I'd sit on my favorite limb;
pick soft pink puffs to buff my nose,
to catch my hair, a crown.
The whippoorwill might come to roost, to sing.
I still climb high when I need someplace to go,
still love things with wings—planes and birds,
giant butterflies and gypsy moths and leaves that spin—
and still have trouble sometimes, coming down.

William T. Delamar

I Cry

I cry
Because children die
While I formulate a wage and salary program.
In a far-off land
Where only hunger holds their hand
Children whimper while I write upon the sand.
The snows are gentle in my night
But cruel to the stretched-out fingers
            of their fright.
Off beyond the haze
Above the tree-line of my gaze
Children stop the search for love and die.
Somewhere are leaves that hide the sun
And rooted paths where children run
And other men who cry,
And do their work
And wonder why.

Thad Stem, Jr.

Unofficial Greeter

When winter came to town at 5:23 last Friday morning
There wasn't any brass band at the courthouse, nor any mayor
To give him the key to our city. There wasn't anyone but me
To say a few frigid words to autumn when she bundled her rags
On a stick, and, turning up her ragged collar, walked slowly
Down the dirt road to Hand-out.

When winter rode up Littlejohn Street, at 5:23,
His white stallion's mane was flecked with ice,
And he routed autumn's pitiful redcoat rear-guard
In the old field where the Opera House once stood.
The fiery neighing of that heavy-footed stallion
Sent tremors as acrobats to scale our walls,
To twirl our steeples as if they were all misty tops.
In the sky two white clouds were fat geese
Running from the plucking wind, and every power line in town
Was a 'cello bleating about hard times and falling weather.

Finally, the sun was a yellow-headed plowboy
Whistling to his team and trying to get his plow-point
Into the frozen rows of daybreak's newgrounds.
I waved my hand in fulsome greeting, and then
I told winter I'd hold his great silver stallion
If he wanted to light and rest.
Having settled another morning and changed another guard
I excused myself and turned another Friday and a winter
To anyone who aspired to be a legatee.

Anna Wooten-Hawkins

Students

Faces like cupped palms.
What would you hide, keep back?
Every year thick as kudzu
they crowd the classroom.
The smallest sprout shows
there is really no death.
Blonde and brazen, who taught you
the summer? Third row, second seat,
somnambulant, don't sleep.
I am the egotistical troll
guarding your semester's castle.
Before you I spangle my talents.
For you my best sterling: fiery
tongue. And in my pockets candy,
stones: seven semi-precious
vocabulary words.
Seven gems I save for you.

Lei Zimmerman

On a Dove's Wings

in the corridor We stood,
my silver wings held your
soft whiteness in a dove's
kiss.
We perched on a park bench,
picked Each other's hearts apart.
and above the veranda-
eclipsed Battery we flew
together.
In the light of a parking lot,
our wings touched, flirted,
tangled among Themselves.

Paul Jones

The Lasting

The flowers, the wine, the common
gifts of love do not linger
like love itself they too
soon find another
cottage like the one we pass
on the way to work
with a garden that tends
its own borders, grass
that limits its height,
and a life so easy it strains
imagination. What lasts
is less cozy, more pervasive;
the sulfur air of a paper
plant that gives a small town
its only hope of growth,
the river that each spring
leaves its bed to visit
the streets of the port,
the long howl coming into the world
to find its hound. The lasting
knows no containment; abandon
is its wild reward.

Salvatore Salerno

A Plate of Bread

Once, swinging on the rocker-chair
that faces woods behind our home,
my daughter and I were still enough to see
a chipmunk scrabble down the woodpile,
nose around, then skitter behind a log.
That caused her to run inside,
fetch a shallow dish and chunk of bread
to feed what she'd seen. I explained
that night was best for shy things,
that a chipmunk won't return
as our neighbor's dog would—
best, then, to leave the bread behind
at the edge of the woods, and hope.

Each day became a ritual
close to the supper hour,
when the long shadows of pines and maples
stretched deep across our lawn,
a ritual of tearing bread
and placing the plate on a stone
for an animal she'd never see again.
This lasted fourteen days, long enough
for her to be enchanted by
her sandbox and swing again,
long enough for its shadow
to stretch across my thoughts.

Not for the impulse of giving food
which, God knows, is common,
nor for the delicate gesture
involved in the breaking of bread,
but for her joy in the simple act,
for not having to *be* there
watching while the gift's enjoyed—
                              yes,
for that, Christina, I am moved
now and at the hour this is read.

Katherine Russell Barnes

Second Child

Passion's first fruit
complete and beautiful
fills, outgrows the bowl
becomes my day
my star

But other nights
refuse a void
and stars take
many forms.

Book XI of Light Food

Men are hunters and fishers, netters and trappers.
And I have been Artemis, wild and virgin
in the sacred places: turning intruders to deer.
A new metamorphosis this time. I am a deer, too.
    You feel the golden arrow in your hide, and are
running, fleeing: anywhere, anywhere *else;* anywhere
safe. It's too late for *safe*. And you know
your arrow hit me. I am a dead deer, too.
                                    Artemis
herself is wounded. That's the difference. The myth
has a different ending this time,
more like the Chinese poem about hunters
invading a countryside, "seducing women"
who are "nourishing spring lusts."
                                    The loss
of privacy then must come. The *private* parts
are full of longing to be changed. Artemis
puts down her bow. Her arrows scatter. She
is naked. Her drops of water change her own
skin, too, to a deer's hide; her hair is light brown
fur; her eyes gentle, pleading. She gives chase.
The dogs are in another part of the forest.
So are the deer the love god sacrificed. You touch
my waist. It only takes one touch to start this
fire that will tremble under our skins
the rest of our lives.

Kathryn Stripling Byer

Weep-Willow
(For Lee)

At night she watched the road
and sang. I'd sigh and settle on the floor
beside her. One song led
to one more song. Some unquiet grave.
A bed of stone. The ship that spun round
three times 'ere it sank,
near ninety verses full of grief.
She sang sad all night long

and smiled, as if she dared me
shed a tear. Sweet Lizzie Creek swung low
along the rocks, and dried beans rattled
in the wind. Sometimes her black dog howled
at fox or bear, but she'd not stop,
no, not for God Himself, not even if he came
astride a fine white horse and bore the Crown
of Glory in his hands. The dark was all
she had. And sometimes moonlight
on the ceaseless water. "Fill my cup,"

she'd say, and sip May moonshine
till her voice came back as strong as bullfrogs
in the sally grass. You whippoorwills
keep silent, and you lonesome owls go haunt
another woman's darkest hours. Clear,

clear back I hear her singing me to sleep.
"Come down," she trolls,
"Come down among the willow
shade and weep, you fair
and tender ladies left to lie alone,
the sheets so cold,
the nights so long."

Nancy Frost Rouse

Words

On secret winter days
my heart anticipates your presence
beyond cold window panes.
Warm, glowing lamplight spills
into the passing days of strangers.
I gather it,
ripe as apples in the snow.
You wait for me—mere breath
holds me in your eyes,
drowning in your voice,
close enough to touch.

Words,
the only gifts we bring,
fill my mind with
sunshine, warming water.
Swans could swim in pools of dreams.
I bite my tongue, ward
off love's faint confessions,
resist the need to pour
myself like oil upon your feet,
sweet wine into your cup—
a hand I cannot hold,
it is not offered me.
I memorize your face, your body,
with my green, green eyes.

Mary Warren-Harris

Storm Clouds

From her kitchen window,
She watches storm clouds gather
Like clusters of dark purple grapes.
She remembers other storms
When angry voices rolled like thunder
And bitterness struck like bolts of lightning.
She lets the dishwater from the sink.

The Green Woman

She should have been serene,
a woman in a pale green sheath,
hair pulled back in a pretty
wreath the color of alfalfa.

She should have bent over the humming
flowerbeds at daybreak, thinned the wide-ranging
iris, bruised in its slipper, pinched back
the red impatiens at her borders, and generally
tidied up. She should have turned away
from the cawing blackbirds and any overly
persistent light—turned toward him
at the window: his lyric sight would be
on her, and on the little girls in their
buttercup leggings, their snug shoes
yielding a little in the dew
as they picked the blue Cupid's dart
and put it in their baskets.

She shouldn't have been this
white thing, worrying words
like beads, hurrying night
to night again, skipping
all the beats. She never
should have missed a
note of the blissful
parrot's song he hummed.

She should have been calm
as kohlrabi, a woman less
patient with unruly florid things,
a woman in a pale green dress.

Benjamin E. Bessette

Duck Decoy   watercolor

Duck Decoy   watercolor

Marcia McCredie

What Dreams? for Bob

You have slept late. The coffee is ready, and I,
for you. Walking gazelle soft, I bring two mugs
to bedside. The mugs steam with smell that is
known to meet us, when each is on the other's
side of sleep.

I am caught in the hold of your sleep-drawn hands. Your
fingers fold into loose fists, but slowly, the smallest
fingers first then finger following finger til your thumbs
deftly latch your new-sculpted grip.

The hands don't relax, but the muscles in your face
slacken softly as white chocolate on a warm day.
You could be holding diamonds, or the shorn locks
of Sampson's hair or fine-formed grains of simple wheat.
Whatever you hold, you have saved from falling.

If I ask you later what you dreamed,
you will say only that you slept well,
your voice falling soft like chips tossed
quickly by a skilled whittler's hand,
away from what takes shape
by the knife and all that forms at
the heart of wood.

I know you can't tell me, even if
the dream has gone with waking or if the words
can only fall, not hold. Awake, you've no patience
with what you haven't claimed. Something in your grain
names me close to you, but strange.

Kay Nelson

Your Scarf

Worn near my cheek,
The fragrance wraps me
Against the chill of your absence.

The fabric, soft as cool fingers
Lingering on wanting flesh,
Soothes my restlessness.

The pattern crosses like our lives,
It's frayed at the end,
Like our love.

Empty coldness still penetrates
The warmth.

Jean Morgan

Leni: Letter from Castle Berg

*"It is perfect here, Princess—everything is...even the housekeeper
Leni, who purveys to all my needs and looks after me so quietly,
silently, almost atmospherically, that I am able to treat her more as a
pleasant climate than as a personification."*
            —Rainer Maria Rilke to Marie Taxis from Schloss Berg am
            Irchel, Canton Zurich, Switzerland, 15 December 1920

The wind curves snow high on the pane;
today the man from the village
had to shovel a path to the door
to deliver the milk and the mail.

Thank you, no, I have no need of a cat.
The fire in the grate speaks to me day and night;
the blizzard makes fine music, better than pianos;
loaves rising in the rack require me constantly, like children.

He in the back room calls out
(not to me, nor in complaint)—the walls echo
his footsteps. How he contends with himself,
like branches wrestling the gale.

Like a currier I comfort and groom, feeling precisely
what to do. I serve his tea in silence,
trailing the warmth of the hearth through draughty halls
from the folds of my skirt.

He is a great man, they tell me, learned
in letters and philosophy; strange I should find him
much like me, long at the windows, thinking
of wind, snow, fire, bread, tea.

Ardis Messick Hatch

Years of Time

"The word 'impossible' is found only in the dictionary of a fool."
—Napoleon

The years between us
catch in my throat
like a knot of grief that won't dissolve.
They make me sick with envy,
immoral with greed.
They make me negotiate with dreams,
bargain with gods you never heard of,
strange beings that do deliver.

The years between us keep me
awake at night counting them past.
They make me empty with hope
strung out like a dry skin.
If you believe in time warp, witches, and spells,
believe in this and don't sleep light.
I would kill to move one of us closer together.

—AND BEYOND

Come, let us walk into April

Virgin Pines   oil

Sam Ragan

Let Us Walk Into April

It was a pear tree in bloom
That lit up your eyes.
You came at blossom time—
Dogwoods and lilacs,
The camellia and azalea,
And the glow of the redbud tree—
Thousands of wildflowers run before your feet,
And a faint green hovers in the woods.
Here we are just before the coming of April,
When the whole world is new
And each day is a beginning,
A time of sunlight and splendor—
Come, let us walk into April.

Ronald H. Bayes

Star With Sun
(after T. Matsuyama)

Look at the sky.
Everyone can see
A pure white star
After a long journey.

Autumn sky afternoon.
Just myself
Looking at
The wideopen white star.

I lie down on the green
Just in front of City Hall.
I desire abundant space more than death.
I seek grandeur of time more than love.

Graceful speech has been asking
And I ask for graceful speech.
My bashful dear, we are only a bashful One.
Why are we shaking like this?

The Star of Abraham has been sent.
The Star of Isaac will be sent.

Well I shall outrun the signal
From the Boy to be a Father—
Listening to it all the way.
Keeping true all the way.

(with Yozo Shibuya)

Passport

His Liberty Bell passport
is an American elegance,
inked and whorled, more beautiful
than Jefferson and Lincoln,
non-negotiable.

Janos locks his door now against Russians,
safe and radared in Carolina swampland,
a citizen of Whiteville, American taxpayer
remembering Hungary,
the passport smooth as a glove in his hand.
He knows what it means
to wake up and speak English.

So, Janos has a claim on bitterness.
Beyond his door, the warm Waccamaw
rolls to shore, and his smooth daughter tans.
She welcomes the air she's hung
with names, American, Hungarian:
she's home among the enemy.

James Applewhite

Light Beyond Thought

I wonder what summer I remember? I
Sit in shadow, where a dust of pollen
On waterfloor moves with the broom of wind.
And gnats gyrate, lighter than dust,
Fluff on the wrist of the river,
Jumping to its pulse. Spider webs float,
Dragonflies chase each other, and the sycamore
Leaning over from the opposite shore,
Its trunk in splotches like quarters,
Like camouflage, is almost silver. Its
Roots exposed by erosion flow
And mold like concrete, a scaffolding
Intricate as water in limestone—
Like the roots of memory. Mountain
Laurel blazes in flower. Green seems
To create its own meaning. This long
Day's sun, still high, seems frozen.
Glistens too richly to question.

Sally Buckner
Mahalia Jackson Gets Ready to Go on Stage

I got a song,
Lord,
I got a song to sing,
to belt to the blue horizon,
to peel the edge off the clouds,
to strike like a slice of lightning, Lord, up there,
my song to drum like thunder,
waking the whole world from slumber,
calling all folk to quiver, Lord,
to quake, to shiver
with fear, with rage, with love, Lord,
with love that lights the sky
and blazes blue in my veins
and curves like the rim of rainbow
and trembles like winds of October
in trees of copper and gold, oh, Lord,
that song going to make all the folks start clapping,
and stomping their happy feet,
and snapping their long strong fingers,
and jumping as straight as arrows,
and singing their hallelujahs,
and staring with great wide eyes, Lord,
gazing in most amazement
at me in my red silk glory,
Lord, Lord, at me.

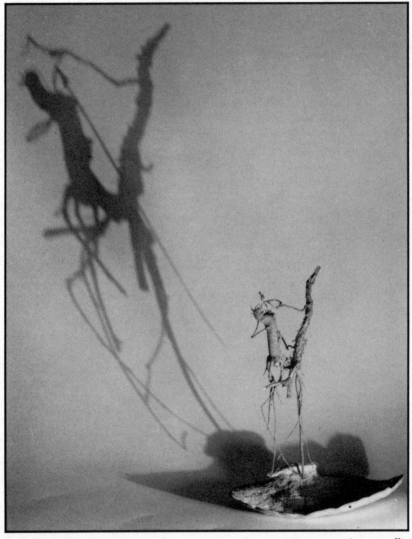

Don Quixote

two roots, a pine needle
and a bracket fungus

Hilda Downer

Shadows that Steep in Dreams of the New Ground

Dream, dream to sleep.
Rock infant softness to our shoulder.
Dream not only of the land we give you,
but of the mountains' blue trill toward worlds.
Dream not only of the river's bordering lace,
but of the gold glint of trout easing a sheer of sun.
Dream not only of the boulder's wrinkled prune shape,
but of its cave's delicate moan of cool air.
Dream not only of the wood's shadows folding light,
but of the walnut's deepest fingernail-press of bark.
Dream not only of the field's claim to smooth green,
but of the wild carrot giving itself to goldenrod and infinite running.
Dream not only of the primitive road's melancholy color,
but of where wild turkey and deer prints mold to fit future walks.
Dream not only of the stream tingling down the slope vertebrae,
but of its bright stone collection and slippery pungence.
Dream not only of the wind thumbing a ball across the yard,
but of branches quietly weighed with the feather sleep of wind.
Dream, dream not only of the distant tree line's serration,
but of eye level pins marching upon the mound of a pin cushion.
Dream, dream, dream not only of the open pond of sky,
but of the clouds signing an interpretation of what the earth smokes.
Dream not only of the land we give you,
the jumbled code of landscape,
but somewhere tagged to your dreams,
allow the essence of what we cannot convey in a poemtime,
the dream of the land we give you.

Fred Chappell

The Watchman

Tonight the Mirror opens up to see
The watchman keeping vigil on the roof
Of the ruining house. The whole long year
He has lain houndlike on his belly
Awaiting the semaphore
Blaze, his hands clenched on the eave, awaiting proof
Of a victory that shall pull down
A proud and bitter family, in rain
Or cold starshine stretched out aloof
To all discomfort, searching the world-rim for a sign.

A thirst is in him for the triumph of his king.
A thirst is in his tribe to know
They shall not heir disgrace
To their children's children, they shall not bow
Their heads before a barbarous race
Who worship alien gods. Though the prophets sing
A harder tragedy to follow
If they win the war, let it still be so.

He is half-crazed with longing. The mountain peak
He stares toward in the reverberant night
Appears and disappears, dark on dark;
Advances upon him, then takes flight
Into the downward-twisting bleak
Futureless whirlpool of aching eyesight.
The stars flitter aimlessly above his head
Like an irritated squad of flies over the dead.

Suppose the message come, the fire leaps red
In the far blackness. Can he still recognize
The signal? So many hours,
So many nights of blankly turning skies
Have darkened his capacities
To understand. The arrow showers
Of meteors no longer startle; he no longer numbers
The falling stars.
The Great Bear lumbers
Over his soul, leaving a shadow like an ebony bruise.

And then
the bruise becomes a pit
That walls him in
So he cannot see out.

Outdoors is Closed
(Lyrics for an original song)

The power plant opened ten years ago,
then closed down nine years ago,
then opened back up eight years ago.
Now everything's all right.
We got plenty of heat and light.

But outdoors is closed.
It's all shut down.
You can't go outside, and walk on the ground.
You've got to stay indoors,
watch the box and meditate.
'Cause if you go outside—you might radiate.
Outdoors is closed; everything's all right;
no more street fights.

I never understood the pandemonium—
it just rained a little plutonium,
dropped iodine on my grapevine;
so now I stock freezer food, Puss and Boots for the cat,
stay inside and get fat.

'Cause outdoors is closed.
It's all shut down.
You can't go outside, and walk on the ground.
You've got to stay indoors,
watch the box and meditate.
'Cause if you go outside—you might radiate.
Outdoors is closed; everything's all right;
no more street fights.

Well it ain't so bad with the trees all gone,
little brown flowers, little brown lawn.
The birds don't sing, but the power lines hum.
It's nice near the plant.
Near the plant's where I'm from.
It's quiet near the plant.
Near the plant's where I'm from.

Guy Owen

My Father's Curse

My father strode in anvil boots
    Across the fields he cursed;
His iron fingers bruised the shoots
    Of green; he stabbed the earth.

My father cursed both sun and rain;
    His sweep cut corn and weed,
And where his fiery plow had lain
    The ruined earth would bleed.

Yet though he raged in bitter brew
    Thick oaths that belled his throat,
God rammed His springing juices through
    And fleshed Himself in fruit.

Judith Holmes Settle

Eyeblink

When I stand, when I
look over the privacy fence,
there is no shadow,
only steady sunlight
bouncing off butterfly wings
and apple tree foliage.

In an eyeblink I can
change my focus,
see sun's ray
or shadow.

Autumn Catalogue

Bravely
as the light flies
I tell you how my heart breaks
for one red maple
on a hill in South Carolina
and for a redtail hawk,
how autumn tramped that country
in dirt feet keening
like an old song. I reason

that things are most themselves
in autumn when at four o'clock
the sun from high cirrus cuts
tall poplars.
Their yellow hands holding the blades
they abide the time
over farms
and country roads. My hand

translucent as I
write by this window
proclaims its architectonic;
tendons slide along the knuckles
gently lift the net of veins
where the life goes home, and I recall
how soft your eyes are sometimes. If

my character likewise
should be exposed,
it would be found a somewhat overbloomed
perpetual. But if found at best
I think I could hollow out my bones,
wait with the redtail hawk
in a known spiral upwards, all
utterance suspended. Glaciers snap.

Quite suddenly
my hair is white—a hawk cries
westward.

Mary B. Preyer

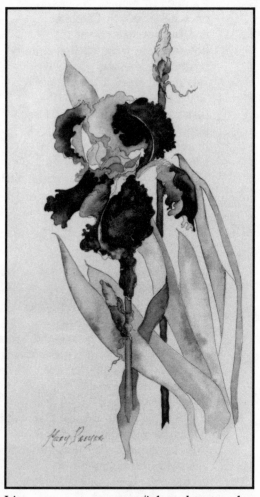

Iris   pen/ink and watercolor

Betty Miller Daly

Acknowledgement

Pink iris opened in the night,
it glistens now from last night's rain.
I search to glimpse its inwardness,
and see enfleshed the involuted
pink of pearl pour from the aureole
and show the traced magenta veins.
The carmine feathered triuned wings
emote, evolve from center out
in rapsody of glory-frills.

I close my eyes and there it is
transcribed inside on softest black.
No wordsmith penned tributes of worth
to this pink sculpted thing so near
to liquid air,
perhaps an angel's thought flown down
from bower of bliss and stilled a day
by special dispensation.
No matter that it fades tonight.

At close of day I still am mute
and so I turn toward west and see
the whole acknowledgement expressed
as entire heaven fires reflect
pure pearl pink with crimson triuned
featured clouds, magenta traced and
centered by the red, red sun;
the iris now is magnified
and magnified.

Grace DiSanto

Less is More
(Triptych)

I.
Far left
in a dusty corner of the Florence Cathedral,
I sit. About me pray God's sheep:
the faithful, the devout: men's heads bowed, sides
of their faces erased by setting sun; women's heads,
mantilla-veiled, their cheeks and brows spidered
by webbing lace. Trying to solve the mystery
I stare up at Michelangelo's *Unfinished Pieta* (Jesus,
His Mary Mother, the Magdalene, Joseph of Arimathea), and
wonder why the stone is undone.

II.
In my dream that night
like the suction fish stuck to a manta ray, I lie
on my stomach, hitching a ride on the back of a flatbet
truck. Over, over, on this driverless carrier, this bullet
train, four tires beat monotonous thump: Rolling over, I
discover six silent lambs (shorn of snouts, mouths, tongues,
their faces end in mailbox slots), looking down on me.
Undone with their odd anatomy, I know, unlike my newborn-son
(he grew the missing flesh between his forefinger and thumb
in days) these lambs won't change.

III.
Next day in the old hills of Fiesole,
I come upon sheep grazing; the nursery rhyme kind, they
baa-baa on grass. ...And, and then, I make the leap:
the sweet unfinished dreamflock and the Holy marble pleased
me more because their faces begged:
Complete me, not with your eyes but with your mind,
the way the blind see.

Bobby G. Price

To the Mistress

To the mistress I never had,
I miss you.
Slinky red or vibrant green
might have flowed from your hips
as they flow from an apple when it's
picked fresh and washed in spring water.
Oh, the crispness of it,
sweet and bitter all at once
like your kisses
(though i never tasted)
I miss them.
Mistress, I miss you
the way I miss an old dog,
long gone from age or automobile—
a friend that curled up, licked my hand,
brought comfort. Comfort.
Demanded nothing, save a little food
and like friendship in return.
Mistress I never had,
Where were you?

Thomas Walters

Tape Wrap
(For James R. VanLaan)

Several volumes might oughta do it the job
"But," you'd laugh with me, "Who the hell'd read 'em?"

To capture verbally a friendship or rarity
The very rarity itself of friendship in a small space
Cannot be done—or
(And here we laugh again) done *well*.

So. In traditional fashion, I refuse to mention the gifts the lifts
The jokes the quests together among musty stacks of books
And stacks likewise of sometimes musty friends too. I won't mention
The in(famous) convertible-top replacement or the
Spontaneous "Que Pasa?" that broke up our girls. Or the
Flavors of beers bought the old wood hauled the insulation inhaled
The other crazies the loving of my daughter Yes the other crazies.

Or your Whitmanian wipes of my fevered fright at Wake in the nights.
("Which I do not forget.")

   Let me, rather, old Meerschaum Man remarkable, share perception
   With you of one act just an-image-really which is
   So by damn symbolic it sounds made up but is not
   Was not. It was:

That Dutch determination had you scrounged on the floor in a corner
      crowded
Of your shamble-staggered paint-smelling office Your business calling
Need of other attentions. Redecoration plans Big things to
Get done all around us.

Yet you hunkered there with my silly headphones faulty
A puzzle a challenge and we
Worked together together together on it
That problem of capricious breakdown way into your night.

110

Still the coupling refused to work.
The sound was a shattered sweetness   distorted.

   Both offended   we wanted the music to come through   by God.

And then   as one   we simplified   snipped the middle coupling out
Like an appendix   like a cancer. Then you sutured, you soldered
Spliced and taped.   Tested.   We
      Grinned at each other over our "Voilas" amid some sweet somewhere
         Violas.

Today, Bless You, I heard Ralph Vaughan Williams' Fifth with tears.
His world of tone and texture between my ears because first you lent
Me the record   But mostly because you would not stop 'til you
Had repaired my twisted line   to Beauty

Thanks is not enough. But it'll have to stand for *this* connection.

R. T. Smith

Night Anthem in West Negril
(for Derek Walcott)

Who is the cricket's kin? Who can live
at his pitch, more vivid than fever, fast
as the green vervain draining hibiscus?
The cicada endures such joy, sings, gives

his shrill evidence. Significant, intense,
he spends his hour in the eucalypt, while
hawk moths hover after the moon, the wily
grassquits skitter amid fireflies, their flints

impotent to hurry dawn. So cicadas chirr
like stars tightening; cricket-pitch, though
the crickets no longer saw their caskets,

and cicadas no longer inhabit theirs.
Philosophers sleep through summer solstice
and miss the meaning, an island's show
of suicide. Ripe mangoes fall and ginger

ripens. To what end all this? Remember
your fury when, young, you stood on a cliff
and wished to be sheer song, thinking, "If...."

Luther Stirewalt

Cloud Passage

Cumulus clouds
dominate the sky
like marble monuments
inscribed with fading runes.
We lie upon the earth
and gaze at unknown symbols.

I once knew a man
who photographed only clouds.
Covering box and head
with black cloth
he pointed an intrusive eye toward heaven
and stopped both wind and cloud
to read the sacred text.

I never saw his photographs.
He died before I knew
the permanence of clouds.

Nina A. Wicker

The Prey

She came sounding a nightingale's wail
A crowline out of West Virginia,
Her beady-eyed flock of seven to rest sunnyside
A Chatham County sedge hill,
The oldest, thirteen, let go campus dreams
Endured himself to farm country, farm folk.
Muscles surging felled trees, axed wood
Hay bales from hot fields.
He horse-talked to thoroughbreds, artistic hands
Patted mares, slabbed his family a cabin
Trapped game to keep them fed.
Red Man bulging his jeans, juicing his grin.

Out of the coal mine, running a downhill chase,
"The old man's a drunk," the neighbors said,
The abandoned miner tracked down his prey—
Open season. His double-barrel blast through
Her bolted door scattered bodies like a covey.
Lawmen downed the wiry hunter.
Neighbors buried the thirteen year old.
"Put him away nice."
Now winter winds whistle the rocks
Smoke curls the boy-laid chimney
And summer breezes echo whippoorwills
Up and down these Deep River hills.

All I Know About Berries

Walking by half-tamed woods, where I'd been a hundred,
a thousand times, I saw a sassafras tree,
a tall one, and hanging over it, a taller
wild cherry. How long since I'd seen wild cherries?
I'd forgotten the taste; the little clusters
were low enough to reach and ripe enough
to try: that unmistakable tang.
Birds get drunk on the berries. Maybe I
got drunk too and didn't even know it.
I learned what to eat and what not to eat
so early I've forgotten how.
I ate mulberries until I was dyed purple.

"Thimbleberries," the woman beside me
at the county market said
in a foreign accent. I wanted to ask her,
what is a thimbleberry, and where are you from?
Instead I looked it up in the dictionary:
raspberries. They grow wild too, in the mountains.
The leather woman who runs the roadside stand
where we stop for the special grapes knew what we wanted.
"They have a kind of a whang to them," she said.
But we were too early, or late, I forget which.
I think the grapes are wild ones, muscadines,
or maybe just gone wild, off on their own.

Blackberries are our berries. They're everywhere.
June bugs will fight you for them.
Picking blackberries, watch out
for bears in the West, in the East,
chiggers, which are more insidious
though not fatal. How long since I've seen
persimmons ripening toward a fall frost?

Character Study   pastel

Julie Suk

Sitting Out a War Once-Removed

It stormed a lot that summer—
brute cloudbursts, pane-rattling thunder.
Open the front door and a bolt might rip
the length of a hall.

It was days of card games and let's pretend,
a battery of rain at the window.

The weeks racked up a list of disasters:
strikes on the golf course,
drownings by undertow.

A man on our block took to his boat
and never returned,
but the war took most,
bit by bit someone,
no one, we knew,
the way ants peel away from remains,
hauling off piecemeal
legs, thorax, wings.

We were left wings, oak leaves, stars,
and a box of photos—a gallery
of uniformed figures in knocked out places
we could only conjure from books.

Villagers, flowers, ruddy cheeks—
what did we know?

Caught in the steady drizzle of our lives,
we hardly looked up from the game
of high-card-take-all.

Leon Carrington Hinton

The Other Side

Five years old again, lost in darkness,
Parents and brothers call
From the other side of the stream,

Richard, Richard! He tries to reach
Them. Hands lunge in the dark.
Each one says, *Take me.*
I'll pull you across.

Just as he touches his father's fingers
He is sucked back into a hole
And falls down, down, down, down.

His seventy-five-year-old emaciated body
Stretches out—a long white ribbon
Under the sheet.

Faces hover. *I thought he was gone.*
His heart did stop.

A prisoner in this clean, well-lit hell
Constantly attacked by white-clad
Grim-faced devils with needles, pills,
Tubes, enemas, robbing him of dignity,

They don't understand
When he talks to people
On the walls and ceiling,

Refuses food and pills, has accidents
And mostly longs
For the other side.

Salieri's Sonnet

Salieri breeds his own cross and crown and composes
in the language of rats in a choir under his earthly
empty seat. Each morning he pleads and prays and weeps
in a human voice unable to accompany thunder, volcanic
wind, heed noise. Salieri breeds his own cross and crown.
Amadeus is born from the pale snake and wicked pig
and he turns to the open window backstage to watch the snow rise
between the fence rail and black hooves. The muse begins
and we call it human as it sleeps and we call it human
as it wakes. Salieri breeds his own cross and crown.
Amadeus hears the singing of the earth men and their ruby dolls.

Ruth Moose

In the Old Camden Market on Main Street
(For Starkey)

There we were in the supermarket of books;
Friends of the Library had stocked
magazines where mushrooms had been,
science fiction between spinach
and bibb lettuce. Ghosts of artichokes
stood on their heads over the gourmet
reading lists. There was fiction
in the meat case. Nabakov with lamb
and veal, Hemingway beside haddock,
Fitzgerald with flounder
and in the wine,
Gertrude Stein. While Alice B.
toiled among the tortes, bread and apple
pies. Where beans had been;
fresh, baked, dried, canned, assorted,
sat National Geographics jungle deep,
waist high. Wildlife swung
on the produce carousel. Paperbacks
filled potato bins. Whodunits did away
with the celery slot. Broccoli and carrots
caught mayhem and murder. In the Laundry,
Travel and Leisure took the aisle.
Cleaning products had Country Life
and frozen foods, how-to-do-its.

Oh Friends, Friends, we wheeled out
shopping bags from Save Rite, Fast Way,
Horn of Plenty. Never have we been
so filled and deliciously fed.

Stephen E. Smith

The Fence

Having sneaked our first cigarettes—
menthol filter-tipped Kools we puffed
like pros beneath a broken moon—
Danny and I found ourselves astride a picket fence
just one block from our empty beds
when a bony blue tick named Duke barked.
He was answered by a sooner in the next county
who awakened a bitch up on Goldsborough Street, etc.,
until the night was a chorus of mongrels gospeling.
Doors and windows jammed open,
lights flooded the darkness, and we sat
trembling astride that fence
not knowing which way to fall.

I tumbled to one side, Danny to the other,
and we lay still as dead men
while flashlights ogled the damp grass,
danced among the limbs of cedars, clattered along
the picket fence just inches above our faces
buried in the fetid glistening of spring onions.
We did not draw breath
until one by one the lights had died,
and the barking trailed into echo.

Later we bragged,
slapped backs and laughed
as we told friends of our escape,
how we'd outwitted man and beast
by just keeping our cool and knowing
that eventually it would all go away,
that no one would remember
those doors thrown open into darkness
or the children we once had been.

Helen M. Copeland

Endangered Specimen

That snake you spared last fall is back.
"Look," you said, spying the hatchling,
"a baby copperhead." With a nudge
from the toe of your boot, it was gone.
Half grown, it watches me from the woodpile
head raised above its bright mosaic coils.

As I walk the path in sandals,
rainwashed roots twist from the ground
and stop me cold, till wood is wood
and I can breathe again. You,
my naturalist son, would smile
at my layman's fantasy.

Yesterday I found snagged on a cedar branch
a loop of tissue skin that bore its print.
How many ghostly membranes will have peeled
from its cool elliptical eyes before
it is thick as the handle of the ax
I keep at the back door?

Shelby Stephenson

When January is Cold

In this ice-edged hour, this January of hogkillings,
I see the whipped creak of trace-chains
slipping under wrinkled snouts, pigs'
lashes like drawn shade-tassels hanging from closed lids,
know the running blood, the trembling
jar of heads and ears on sleds muledrawn to the barrel
sliced in two bubbling with scalding water
triple rainbows in the sun—
I believe in the first
dying, feel the goneness, the sacrifices
piling up in the fire growing around the lightwood
knots under the vat, the ice melting in dribs down
hanging trees,
the washed-in-and-out of things in a January
coming onto an old gallows tree when hogs are shot,
cleaned and carved and salted in a box or hung up to the ceiling
in smokehouses on nails and wires to cure,
tongues dripping.

Sister Bernetta Quinn, O.S.F.

Verse Letter

Chuck Sullivan, strong Gaelic sea-surge name,
And you, strong Gaelic sailor-son of God,
Friend of the saints you most resemble: Peter,
Teresa, Saint Don Bosco. Francis? Well,
Perhaps not Francis, Chuck. But wait a while.

Are you aware, Chuck, how you fan the flame
Flickering in your fellow poets' hearts,
How your Samantha, Sean believe the gospel
"According to Chuck" reborn in your soul's cell,
You Irishman with that amazing smile?

What if you enter heaven deaf, lame,
Eyeless? Let "Revelation" trace the arc:
Leaping and shouting, you—*numero uno*—
Will lead us like Hart's wildly ringing bell,
You Israelite in whom there is no guile.

What do your gifts mean, Sullivan? What blame
Must you endure should you deny the power
Of drawing pilgrims to the running waters
Where they can drink their peace, learn the godspell,
Doomed without you to deserts mile on mile?

They mean, when the road forks you take the same
Sharp-stoned cross-ending turn your Brother took
When many walked with him no longer. Jesus
Needs you to sing his truth, to laugh his will,
To weep his tears, to play his knight in style.

Keep the Faith, catechist Chuck Sullivan;
Pay the high price of love, embrace your night,
Alone yet not alone, not one but two.
Sullivan, Christ will tell you what to do,
Simply, each morning, like the morning light.

Maureen D Sutton

High Noon at the Matinee

If you ask me, I'm a feminist.
Why then, again

thirty years later with
children in my lap and
Tex Ritter modulating my heartbeat
do I sit through "High Noon"
like a parched twelve-year-old
lapping Gary Cooper's eyes
like Texas deep-well water?

When Grace Kelly pleads,
"Why must you go back to town
and face Frank Miller's gang?"
my stoic Cooper straight-lips it,
"If you don't know, I can't explain it"—

the very thing
you don't say to a feminist—
and I just love it and think how perfect.

I've self-injected Steinem and Jong
Friedan and Beauvoir. Still no immunity
against a-man's-gotta-do
what-a-man's-gotta-do

and when Cooper drills Miller,
me and the kids whoop like Comanches
and he could track Hadleyville dust
through my bedroom anytime.

Am I still stuck
in the Great Dismal Swamp
of the '50's

or is it that lady Grace,
the Coop's Quaker bride, finally
backshoots the bad guy?

Richard DeLos Mar

Harbor

The night my grandfather died,
I smoked my first cigarette
squatting on hay
musty as a root cellar.
Outside, hogs
panted in their pens,
and far off the moonlight
glistened on miles of old fence.

That night at the hospital,
his oxygen tent
billowed like a sail,
hoses mooring him to his bed.
I waited, listening
to the plastic bellows
and counted, remembering
his breath rising like smoke,
cold over the corn stalks.

Joanna Allred McKethan

Sacred Shadows

She should have breathed.

She should have lifted up the corners
of yellowed, crocheted lace
and dusted more than dust away.
She should have let the sunlight in
instead of drawing heavy drapes....

But Grandma was sacred
and what she did was, too.
Even her gory rites of purification
became stakes of true religion...
to bless Grandma's wrongs
she twisted all she knew of right,
askew.

Just one piercing shaft of sunlight
and Grandma's image
would have turned to clay
and Aunt could have walked away....

She could have breathed.

Stephen Morris Roberts

October Shadows

Your granddad built highways.
The last time I called
your mom had died.

One night your uncle drove me
in his jeep, headlights searching
the fields for deer.

You and I agreed my calling
would stop. I don't remember
your daughter's name.

Dean M. Hale

O.R. Mask

Whistling,
bursting through the swinging door,
surgeon's cap cocked over his left eye,
his tunic blood-spattered green,
he swaggers from the O.R.

"How did it go?" I ask.

He grins.

"Seven hours on the table,
and the old crock died.
But what the hell...
'Can't win 'em all."

I stiffen, wheel away. Escape.

But I have left my specimens behind.
I hesitate...turn back...
then crack the door.

And there...alone,
his forehead jammed against the tile,
he beats and beats a fist
against the wall.

Passiflora
(To Paul)

You walk on shorebird legs
    fingering shells in moist sand
You examine each hammock plant
    root, stem, leaf, flower
    and know its whole name
You count petals
    dissect anther and pistil
    brush pollen grains here to there
You play violin pacing the length of the house
    late at night
    play psaltery and mandolin like a medieval minstrel
Alone, wanting to be alone with your
    passions

But what of this unnamed friend?
Just a friend, you say
You help her with her children now and then
Three of them
    two blond, blue-eyed girls near adolescence
    and the baby
        fragile, thin
        with dark eyes and tracing fingers
Did your friend offer one passion in hope of sharing
    all the others?
She must not know
    you keep the curtains drawn
    and wash your windows
    at night

Pamolu Oldham

Cameron '85

When the Mexicans work here
they leave old shoes in the yard
and on the table out front
hot peppers, red and green,
like a hundred fingers.

Ruby P. Shackleford

The Drums Come

The drums come
on leaden feet
the horns are windy toes
violins flow under agile fingers

That music is childhood's world—
a house of tangled sticks
mental after-burn

The strains dredge up from memory
the injustice of one spring day
a friend conceived a prank for us
then became the accuser
her scheming
robbed that neighbor's pansy bed
not my small fingers

But the lashes you laid
on my innocent flesh
couldn't comprehend
the word:
"Hypocrite"

Ann Deagon

Claiming the Body

Corpus delicti, my
student pointed out,
differs only a hair
from *corpus dilecti,*
the beloved's body
from the corpse.

Do not wait for the coroner's call.
Do not rely on dental records
or what the subject wore when last seen.
Even the mole under the left breast
(nursing one infinitesimal and silken hair)
is inconclusive. The braided scars
at calf and chest where surgeons ripped
a vein to splice into the plugged heart
are undistinguished. We are all
imperfect. We all have gone
under the knife. How shall you know
your true love from another, after
the death squads come?

                    Anticipate.
Remark what qualities no undertaker
(even in the Regime's employ) can sham:
the staunch tongue that speaks love
clearer than words. The tenor cry
that breaks the throat to resonate
in the great fleshed skull. The eyes,
how blue they glare out of their wrinkled den.
How from under the thick cuticle
unmanicured, rises the moon.
Do not wait. Rely on nothing.
Claim the body now.

Poets

Betty Adcock is Kenan Writer-in-Residence at Meredith College in Raleigh. She has published *Walking Out*, and *Nettles*, which won the Roanoke-Chowan Award. Recent work appears in *Georgia Review, Kenyon Review,* and *Southern Review.*

Andrew J. Angyal is an Associate Professor of English at Elon College.

James Applewhite was born in Stantonsburg, NC and attended Duke University where he now teaches. His *Ode to the Chinaberry Tree and Other Poems* won the 1986 Roanoke-Chowan Award. *River Writing, An Eno Journal* will be published in 1987.

Calvin Atwood, author of *A Squadron of Roses* lives in Atlanta with his wife, Carol Ann. He served twice as president of the North Carolina Poetry Society and is currently president-elect of the Georgia State Poetry Society.

Margaret Boothe Baddour has poems published in many magazines and anthologies, most recently *Stone Country* and *Blue Pitcher.* She is Vice President of NC Writer's Network; Editor of NC Women's Expressions Series, St. Andrews Press.

Wilma Loeschen Barefoot lives in the country with husband M.B. Barefoot. Family, church, and community activities engage all of her days at this time. Reading, cooking and gardening are her hobbies.

Katherine Russell Barnes is a wife, mother, grandmother, and nurse. She has a continuing love/hate affair with words. Her poems have been published in *Crucible, Pembroke Magazine,* and *Dragonfly.*

Ronald H. Bayes of St. Andrews College has lived in Japan on several occasions, and read at the first Japan-International Poetry Festival in 1987.

Mae Woods Bell is the author of *WRYmes* (St. Andrews College Press), and is an award-winning columnist, humorist and book critic. She was president of NC Writers' Conference; she also conducts a community college writers' workshop.

Kate Blackburn writes poetry, fiction, and drama and teaches journalism. Her work has appeared in Canada, England, Scotland, and here in the States. ''I am a grandmother, a traveler, and an optimist, roughly in that order.''

Will Blythe grew up in Chapel Hill. He has published fiction and reviews, and works now for *Esquire.*

James Boyd wrote short stories, poems, and novels including *Old Pine and Other Stories,* published posthumously in 1952, and his famous novels: *Drums, Marching On, Long Hunt, Roll River,* and *Bitter Creek.* He died in 1944.

Sally Buckner of Raleigh teaches at Peace College and co-directs the Capital Area Writing Project. Publications include articles, plays, stories, poems in many periodicals, and a poetry collection, *Strawberry Harvest.*

Kathryn Stripling Byer lives in Cullowhee with her husband and daughter. Her first book, *The Girl in the Midst of the Harvest* was published last year in the AWP Award Series. Her second book *Wild Wood Flower* is forthcoming.

Mary Belle Campbell, creative writing instructor, Sandhills Community College uses

Jung's "active imagination" and dream recall to stimulate greater awareness of one's storehouse of creative images. She has a book and two manuscripts.

Joel Chace currently teaches English at Mercersburg Academy in southern Pennsylvania. He has published poems in various magazines and journals. His first book, *The Harp Beyond the Wall,* was published in 1984 by Northwoods Press.

Fred Chappell teaches at the University of North Carolina at Greensboro. *The Fred Chappell Reader* appeared in 1987 from St. Martin's Press.

Shirley Graves Cochrane has published *Burnside,* and *Family and Other Strangers.* Her poetry and fiction have appeared in *The International Poetry Review, Belles Letters,* and *Mississippi Review.* She lives in Washington, D.C.

Claire Cooperstein of Chapel Hill has had poems published in *The Lyricist, Cairn, Rhino,* and as prize winners in *Crucible* and *Amelia Magazine.* Her work has appeared frequently in the NC Poetry Society's *Award Winning Poems.*

Helen M. Copeland, a "lay naturalist," has published four children's books, and short stories in numerous magazines. She has recently completed an adult novel. Her collection of poems will be published by St. Andrews Press.

Emily Sargent Councilman is a Past-Chairman of the Poetry Council of North Carolina, currently a member of the Poetry Society of America, the NC Writers' Conference, Poetry Society of NC, and consultant for the Burlington Writers Club.

Betty Miller Daly received many awards and prizes for her poetry and short stories. She published *As A Woman Thinketh,* and *Sandscript.* She served as president of the NC Poetry Society. In 1982 she died at the age of 56.

Barbara Rosson Davis is one of the founders of *Poetry Center Southeast* at Guilford College. She has poems in several publications including *International Poetry Review,* and *Carolina Quarterly.*

Irene Dayton is author of: *In Oxbow of Time's River, Seven Times The Wind, The Panther's Eye,* and *The Sixth Sense Quivers.* She has published in literary journals in the US, Europe, and Japan, and is working on her second novel.

Ann Deagon, writer in residence at Guilford College and Director of Poetry Center SE, works in both poetry and fiction. Her last novel was *The Diver's Tomb;* and *The Polo Poems* is forthcoming from the University of Nebraska-Omaha 1988.

Gloria Delamar is the author of scholarly refrence books (*Curiosities of Mother Goose; Round Re-Soundings; Children's Rhymes and Rhythms*), features, op-eds, and poetry. She teaches writing and creativity techniques.

William Delamar is a hospital administrator who writes poetry, and has written and/or edited technical articles and manuals. He is currently working on a mainstream novel.

Rebecca McClanahan Devet is Poet-in-Residence for Charlotte-Mecklenburg Schools. Her poems appear in *Carolina Quarterly, Pembroke Magazine,* and others. University Presses of Florida published her book of poems, *Mother Tongue.*

Grace DiSanto has two collections of poetry (both published by Briarpatch Press, Davidson): *The Eye Is Single,* winner of the Oscar Arnold Young Memorial Cup, 1982, and *Portrait of the Poet as Teacher: James Dickey,* 1986.

Harriet Doar of Charlotte, a former newspaper writer, has published poetry, fiction and articles in magazines and anthologies. She is the author of a volume of poems, *The Restless Water*, published by St. Andrews Press.

Hilda Downer, presently a graduate student at ASU, lives in Boone with her husband, Bruce Richter, and son Branch. She is the author of one book, *Bandana Creek*. She is currently finishing a novel.

Ann Dunn, poet and dancer, has toured her programs, a complex texture of word and movement image, in 17 states and Italy. Her poems, plays, and critical articles have appeared in journals, anthologies and newspapers across the US.

Clyde Edgerton is the author of *Raney* and *Walking Across Egypt*, both novels. He lives in Durham and teaches at St. Andrews College in Laurinburg, NC. "Outdoors Is Closed" is sung on the album and tape "Walking Across Egypt."

Grace Ellis is a teacher and playwright living in Moore County. The poem included in this anthology is adapted from her play, "The Hidden Treasure of Moore."

Rebecca J. Finch was graduated from UNC-G in 1970. She taught for several years and has a lab to clone plants *in vitro* for the family nursery in Bailey, NC. Her poems and articles have appeared in various publications.

Charles Fort is Director of the Creative Writing Program and Associate Professor of English at the University of North Carolina at Wilmington. He is the author of *The Town Clock Burning*, St. Andrews Press, 1985.

Grace L. Gibson teaches at St. Andrews Presbyterian College. She has two books of poetry, *Home In Time* (1977) and *Drakes Branch* (1982). She is at work on a prose collection.

Marie Gilbert of Greensboro is the author of *From Comfort* and *The Song and The Seed*, both from Green River Press, University Center, Michigan.

Anna-Carolyn Stirewalt Gilbo is author of *I Hate You! Love, Don*. She has published in *Hyperion, Soundings in Poetry, St. Andrews Review,* and others. She is active in several writing groups and is working on her second novel.

Elaine L. Goolsby was born on a NC tobacco farm, and lives in Durham. A wife, mother, social worker, and writer of poetry, journals, and letters, she is currently working on a manuscript of letters.

Margaret A. Graham is author of 9 books. She is currently working on a novel, *Anna*, and Harper & Row will release *Resurrection Stories* and *Miracle Stories* in 1988. Works in progress are *Faith Stories* and *Vision Stories*, Harper & Row.

Elinor Owens Gray is a member of The Burlington Writers Club, The Poetry Society of America, and The North Carolina Poetry Society, Inc. She has been published in national magazines and anthologies. She has a novel, *Mizz*.

Dean M. Hale is a retired medical laboratory supervisor. He lives in North Carolina.

Bobby Sidna Hart, a Weymouth Writer-in-Residence 1986-1987, writes poetry, essays and short stories. "Carolina Mountain Man" appeared in *Signs Along The Way* (NCPS Anthology 1986). She is a member of the NC Writer's Network.

Ardis Messick Hatch, a poet, critic and writing teacher for 20 years, is well-known in the PITS Program, and is a master teacher on The National Humanities Faculty. Her books include *The Illusion of Water* and *To Defend A Form*.

Gwyn Harris, a native of Laurinburg and graduate of Duke University, is now a graduate student at Pembroke State University. A high school English teacher, she has two sons and is "a lover of nature, travel, and words."

Tom Hawkins has published poetry and stories in literary magazines including *Intro, Ploughshares, Carolina Quarterly, Greensboro Review, Poetry Australia,* and *Kansas Quarterly*. His book of short stories will be published soon.

Leon Carrington Hinton, a Burlington poet and short story writer, is past president of the North Carolina Poetry Society, on the boards of the NC Writer's Network and the Poetry Council of NC. He has published in anthologies.

Judy Hogan lives in Saxapahaw and is editor/publisher of The Carolina Wren Press. Her third book is *Susannah, Teach Me To Love/Grace, Sing To Me*. She teaches free classes for writers in the Durham and Burlington libraries.

Lois Holt has published in *International Poetry Review, Crucible, Pembroke Magazine* and *Portfolio, 1983*. Her work has appeared in several anthologies: *Writer's Choice, New NC Poetry: The Eighties,* and *Signs Along the Way*.

Lorraine Hueneke is a native of New England and she has lived in North Carolina 20 years. This, her first published poem, was written at Weymouth in 1985. She has had articles published in *The State Magazine, Charlotte Observer,* and *NC Catholic*.

Gladys Owings Hughes is president of the North Carolina Poetry Society. Her poems have been published in state and national magazines and anthologies.

Ellen Turlington Johnston-Hale, Poet-in-the-Schools, consultant, and author of five books of poetry, has a PBS series, "Poetry Alive" that airs nationally. Her poems have appeared in *St. Andrews Review, The Lyricist,* and *Crucible*.

Paul Jones, a systems programmer, lives with a classical archaeologist and two Turkish Salukis. He is past winner of NCAC Fellowship, Carolina Quarterly Prize, Southern Humanities Review Prize, and co-editor of *Cardinal*.

Susan B. Katz is a Raleigh journalist, columnist, and poet whose work has appeared in *The Kansas Quarterly, St. Andrews Review, Pembroke Magazine, Woman's Day, The Spectator, Southern Magazine,* and elsewhere.

Mary Kratt is a Charlotte, NC poet with poems in *Stone Country; Tar River Poetry; Kansas Quarterly;* and *Chattahoochee,* a collection from Briarpatch Press, 1982; and four non-fiction books.

E. Waverly Land lives in Arlington, Virgina. He is a budget officer for the Office of the Secretary of the US Department of Health and Human Services. He is a graduate of St. Andrews College and has lived on the Outer Banks of NC.

Julian Long was Executive Director of the Sandhills Arts Council 1974-1980 and is now at North Texas State University's Center for Texas Studies. His poems, articles and review have appeared widely.

Virginia Love Long has released six volumes, including *Letters of Human Nature,* with Rochelle Holt, which was a 1985 Pulitzer nominee in the Small Press Prose Division.

She resides in her native Person County with her mother.

Mitchell Forrest Lyman was reared in Tidewater Virginia, and has lived in Florida, Maryland, and California before moving to Chapel Hill in 1968. She is a daughter, wife/widow, mother, neighbor, citizen...and poet-by-compulsion.

Richard DeLos Mar has poetry in anthologies and journals including the *New York Poetry Anthology, Manna,* and *North Carolina's 400 Years: Signs Along the Way.* He is a member of several writers organizations.

Marcia McCredie, a Raleigh resident, works as a technical writer for Telex Computer Products. She has recently published in *The Arts Journal* and *Wolphen Branch.*

Agnes McDonald teaches English at UNC-Wilmington. Her poems have appeared in a number of literary magazines and *Four North Carolina Women Poets* in 1982. She writes fiction, essays and articles on the teaching of writing.

Michael McFee, visiting Poet-in-Residence at Cornell for 1986-87, received a fellowship in creative writing from the NEA for 1987-88. His first book of poems was *Plain Air.* His poems have appeared in many publications.

Sam McKay is a Presbyterian minister who occupies himself with many interests including poetry and photography. He is a past president of NCPSI, is active in several poetry groups, and lives with his wife, Martha, in Broadway.

Joanna Allred McKethan has published poems in *The Lyricist, Crucible,* and *Sanskrit.* Of 12 poems chosen for *Fields of Earth Forum,* over half won prizes. A prize winning water colorist, she exhibits in major shows in NC and SC.

Heather Ross Miller, winner of the 1983 North Carolina Medal for Literature, has published eight books of fiction and poetry. She teaches in the University of Arkansas MFA program.

Shirley Moody has been active as a poet in the NC Artist-in-Schools program since 1979. She was one of *Four NC Women Poets,* St. Andrews Press, 1982, and has a forthcoming volume, *Charmers,* from St. Andrews Press in 1988.

Ruth Moose has published *To Survive,* and *Finding Things In The Dark.* She has short stories in *Atlantic Monthly, Redbook, Greensboro Review,* and a collection, *The Wreath Ribbon Quilt.* She is poetry editor of *The Arts Journal.*

Jean Morgan, born in Lancaster County, Pa, now lives in Charlotte, NC. She teaches at Queens College and works as a visiting artist in the Carolinas. Jean read "Leni" March 29, 1987, at the Library of Congress.

Kay Nelson is a past president of the Burlington Writers Club, a member of the NC Poetry Society, and serves as secretary on the Board of Directors of Alamance County Arts Council. Her work has appeared in the *Wayah Review.*

Sallie Nixon, teacher and poet, is a native of Henderson who lives in Lincolnton. Two collections, journals, anthologies, and textbooks carry her work. A University of Nebraska Phi Beta Kappa, she has won national and state honors.

Maud R. Oaks, a past president of the NC Poetry Society, is a member of that group and of the Burlington Writers Club. She lives in Burlington, NC with her husband, Charles, and has a daughter, Laura Oaks, of Hillsborough.

Pamolu Oldham has published in *Agora, Love Stories By New Women, The Columbia Review, Ink, The Arts Journal, Crane's Creek Review, Luna Tuck,* and *The Southern Poetry Review.* She is Co-Editor of *Old Age Ain't For Sissies.*

Lu Overton, a native of Wadesboro, has degrees in journalism and English. Her poems have been published on local, state, and national levels; her feature stories in leading daily papers. She is currently writing and teaching.

Guy Owen was teacher, editor, writer, and founder of *Southern Poetry Review.* He was awarded the Sir Walter Raleigh and NC Award in fiction, and the Roanoke-Chowan in poetry. He married Dorothy Jennings, and had two sons.

Cindy Paris lives and works in Durham. Her poems have previously been published in *Poetry East, Carolina Quarterly, Piedmont Literary Review, Plainsong, Cresent Review, Plains Poetry Journal,* and *Blue Pitcher.*

Constance Pierce has a short story collection, *When Things Get Back to Normal,* and a chapbook, *Philippe At His Bath.* Recipient of an NEA fellowship, she is in the English Department at Miami University in Oxford, Ohio.

Bobby G. Price is a native of Goldsboro, NC. His chapbook, *Strangulation,* won the 1983 Bunn-McClelland Memorial Chapbook Award. He has a full-length volume of poetry, *Visualize* and was at the Atlantic Center for the Arts in Florida.

Reynolds Price, James B. Duke professor of English at Duke University, has published six novels, two collections of short stories, two collections of poems, a collection of essays, and two plays during his career spanning three decades.

Sister Bernetta Quinn has just finished *Pilgrimage To The Stars: Kingdom Inferno, I,* a young person's guide to *The Divine Comedy,* on which she has been working steadily since she taught the epic at St. Andrews College in 1982.

Sam Ragan, Poet Laureate of North Carolina, is Director of the Writers-in-Residence Program at Weymouth. He has published four books: *The Tree in the Far Pasture, To The Water's Edge, Journey Into Morning,* and *A Walk Into April.*

Sandra Redding is a grandmother and student in the MFA Creative Writing Program at UNC-Greensboro. Currently, she is working on a novel.

Stephen Morris Roberts grew up in Winston-Salem. He received his BA at UNC-Chapel Hill, and his MA at Hollins College. He is currently a teaching assistant in the MFA Program in creative writing at George Mason University.

Nancy Frost Rouse, of Lucama, received her BA in English from Atlantic Christian College. Her poems have appeared in various NC publications. In 1987 she was awarded the Poet Laureate Award of the NC Poetry Society.

Anne Russell is a journalism professor at Pembroke State University. Her play "The Porch" was produced in Greenville, Raleigh, and Cincinnati. Her book of poetry *Sketches* is set at Wrightsville Beach, where she lives.

Rebecca Ball Rust is founder of the NC Haiku Society and author of the books *The Outside of Haiku, I Remember Morehead,* and *Tu-Tu, The Would-Be Ballerina.* Her prose and poetry have been published in the U.S.A., Japan, and Canada.

Salvatore Salerno teaches English at UNC-G and NC A&T University. He has been published in such magazines as *Descant, Poem, Greensboro Review*, and *Wormwood Review*. He was a poet and playwright in the NC Visiting Artist Program.

Judith Holmes Settle started writing and publishing poetry a year shy of her fiftieth birthday. Since then she has included fiction and non-fiction, discovering that in the fullness of time she can do things she never dreamed.

Ruby P. Shackleford is a retired professor of English at Atlantic Christian College, and past president of NC Poetry Society. Her publications include: *Dreamer's Wine, Poems, Visual Diary, Poems 4, Ascend The Hill*, and *Bamboo Harp*.

R.T. Smith is Poet-in-Residence at Auburn University. His newest book is *Birch-Light* (Tamarack Editions).

Stephen E. Smith is the author of *The Bushnell Hamp Poems, The Great Saturday Night Swindle* (Stories), and *Honeysuckle Shower and Other Parables*. He lives in Southern Pines.

Mary C. Snotherly, Writer-in-Residence for Wake County Arts Council, on the Board of Directors for NCWN, Chairman of NC Writers' Conference, publishes in *Pembroke, Four NC Women Poets, Southern Poetry Review*, and *Arts Journal*.

Thad Stem, Jr., native of Oxford, NC, published seventeen books of poetry and prose including *The Jackknife Horse*, winner of the Roanoke-Chowan Award, and *Spur Line. Journey Proud* is a volume of selected poems. He died in 1980.

Shelby Stephenson was born in Johnston County, NC. He has published two chapbooks, *Middle Creek Poems* and *Carolina Shout!* He is Professor of English at Pembroke State University, where he edits *Pembroke Magazine*.

Lee Steuer was born in 1958 in Mt. Pleasant, SC, and is a life long resident of South Carolina. He now lives and writes in Spartanburg, SC.

Luther Stirewalt is a retired professor of Classical Languages and New Testament Literature. He and his wife have built their own home, where he continues writing and publishing poetry and articles on ancient letter writing.

Juli Suk, Associate Editor of *Southern Poetry Review*, has had poems appear in *Embers, Montana Review, Visions*, and *Zone 3*. She was a prize winner in the *Devil's Millhopper* poetry competition.

Maureen D Sutton has poetry in *Pembroke Magazine, The Cape Rock, Sandhills Review, San Fernando Poetry Journal, Up Against The Wall*, and *Crane's Creek Review*. She is a member of the NC Writer's Network, and the NC Poetry Society.

Sally Svee, a member of Burlington Writers, NCPS, and the NC Writer's Network, has received awards in poetry and fiction, and been published in *Wayah Review, Bay Leaves, Signs Along the Way*, and *O. Henry Festival Stories* (1987).

Hazel Foster Thomas, author of *Under Papa's Oak Tree* has published in more than a dozen magazines, anthologies, and papers. She is a native of Sanford, NC, and says she likes to write from experience best.

Kate Kelly Thomas returned to poetry after her children were grown and educated. Her work is published in various magazines and anthologies. Kate is a native Tarheel and lives near Sanford, North Carolina.

Thomas Walters, a poet, novelist, and painter, was professor of English at NCSU from

1964 until his death in 1983. His works include *Always Next, Seeing in the Dark,* and *Randolph Bourne—An American Radical.*

Marsha White Warren, Associate Editor of the NCPS's *Signs Along The Way,* has lived in North Carolina since 1961. Her poems appear in three anthologies. She has a children's novel, *Josie,* in progress.

Mary Warren-Harris is a reporter on *The Pilot* and lives in Southern Pines. She has published in several magazines over the years.

John Foster West is a professor of English at Appalachian State University. Author of two novels and three books of poetry, his novel, *Time Was,* was a candidate for the Pulitzer Prize.

Reed Whittemore is the Poet Laureate of the state of Maryland and was twice a poetry consultant to the Library of Congress. An award winning poet, he has won many prizes for his poetry.

Nina A. Wicker of Sanford, North Carolina has chosen grandchildren, camping, writing, and the study of poetry to fill her retirement years. Her collector's item of Haiku, *October Rain on My Window,* was published in 1984.

Emily Herring Wilson is a teacher at Salem College.

Anna Wooten-Hawkins has published poetry and poetry criticism in numerous magazines, journals, and anthologies. Her chapbook *Satan Speaks of Eve In Seven Voices, After the Fall* was published by the NC Writer's Network (1986).

Lisa-Catherine Yost is a senior at Appalachian State University. She has published in *Awarding Winning Poems, The Pilot,* and *North Carolina's 400 Years: Signs Along the Way.* She is the Associate Editor of *Cold Mountain Review.*

Lei Zimmerman is a graduate of St. Mary's College in Raleigh, NC, and is presently attending the College of Charleston. She has been writing poetry and fiction for several years.

Artists

Benjamin E. Bessette is best known as the manager and Maitre d' of Sleddon's Restaurant in Southern Pines. His painting is limited to an occasional course at Sandhills C.C., and in Marblehead during the summer closing of Sleddon's.

Thomas E. Culbreth grew up in Southern Pines. Since graduating from NCSU in 1965 in Product Design, he has worked in Industrial Design and Graphics in both this country and Australia. He is currently working in advertising.

Danila Devins, primarily a portrait artist, specializes in dogs and horses. She studied at the Institute of Art, Florence, Italy, and Ringling School of Art, Florida. She has exhibited in the Republic of Panama, Canal Zone, and Italy.

Arthur Frank studied in France and continued in the vein of French Impressionism. A particularly fine landscape artist, he has left some paintings of Maine where he summered. He was a contemporary and friend of James Boyd.

Maureen Frederick received her art degree from London University in England. Currently living in Pinehurst, she has taught Batik and Textile Design in Iran, and has exhibited Batiks and Watercolors in Iran, Spain, the UK, and the US.

Ann Listokin is a composer, pianist, and teacher. She has composed music for chorus, theater, voice, solo instruments, string quartets, and other chamber groups. Her music has been performed in America and Europe.

Meredith Martens studied at the Corcoran School of Art, San Francisco and Maryland Art Institutes, and her exhibitions include Palm Beach and Paris. Painting famous race horses (including *Secretariat*) is her specialty.

Mary Katherine Philipp is currently pursuing a career in medicine. She has had an exhibit of her sketches at Duke University and has won several awards for her art work. She enjoys working in pencil and oil.

Mary B. Preyer of Southern Pines, a B.F.A. in Interior Design from UNC-G, has served on the Editorial Staffs of McCalls and Modern Bride. Working in pencil, pen and ink, and watercolor, she specializes in flower paintings.

Richard Munger Preyer won the *National Scholastic Art Award First Prize in Oil* while still in high school. A graduate of UNC and the Phoenix School of Design in NY, his paintings ranged from outdoor scenes to portraits.

Jody Scott, originally from PA, has lived in NC for eleven years. In 1982 he opened his own graphic design studio in Southern Pines. His paintings have appeared in shows in PA and NC. Lewis Dillon assisted with this picture.

Susan Carlton Smith, of Durham, is Conservator of the DUMC Library. A professional illustrator of botanical journals, she has illustrated two children's books, and *Wildflowers of NC*. Her work is known internationally.

Catharine Callaway Stirewalt graduated from Duke in 1971 as a painting major. She now designs and makes jewelry, for which she has won several awards. She lives in Hillsborough, NC.

Nancy Williams has exhibited her watercolor, acrylic, and egg tempera paintings throughout the US. Her subjects vary from wildlife and landscapes, to portraits. This prize-winning artist is currently painting in Alaska.